Dr Davies, his book

Dr Davies, his book

compiled by
Sylvia Davies, Linda Hawkes, Doris Irving,
Margaret Lloyd and Carole Oliver

Logaston Press

LOGASTON PRESS
Little Logaston Woonton Almeley
Herefordshire HR3 6QH
www.logastonpress.co.uk

First published by Logaston Press 2009
Copyright © Logaston Press on behalf of the contributors

ISBN 978 1906663 24 7

Set in Minion by Logaston Press
and printed in Great Britain by Bell & Bain, Glasgow

This book is published in aid of the Gurkha Welfare Trust, as Dr Brian Davies ('the Doc' to so many, and Major Davies to his Gurkha regiment in the Second World War) would have wished, and all profits will be donated to the Trust. We are delighted to have received good wishes for this publication from Joanna Lumley, who has done so much to help and support the Gurkhas.

Contents

Foreword

At the funeral service held for Dr Brian Davies in St Edward's Church Knighton in January 2009, over 600 people were present. Someone said, 'Everyone here must have a story about the Doc', and this simple sentence sparked an idea for a book of memories of and tributes to Dr Davies.

I feel very privileged to have asked to write this foreword, and to be part of the small group set up to plan the book. along with Sylvia Davies, Linda Hawkes, Margaret (Maggie) Lloyd and Carole Oliver. Over the last few months we have met at my home for tea, cake and reminiscences, and so the book was born.

Our contributors have been many and varied, and for that we thank them. We thank also Peter and Annette Baker at the Bookshop in Knighton for being a post office for contributions, and Graham Benbow for supporting us from the start, with encouragement and material that he had collected whilst the Doc was alive. Many thanks also to Liz Trow for her super drawings, and to Linda Hawkes for the little sketches used between contributions; both add so much to the finished book. We are grateful to Mrs Lockey for supplying photographs and for telling us about an article written by BCD for *The Sirmooree* (the Gurkha magazine), and to the publishers of *The Sirmooree* for allowing us to print this little known autobiographical gem. Thanks as well to Andy and Karen Johnson of Logaston Press for guiding and advising us (and improving my map reading skills trying to find them).

Robert and I have been friends of BCD for 35 years and have felt grateful to have been able to be there for him in his later years. It was a pleasure and joy to know him and his wife Alison. God Bless you, Brian, and your honey pot.

Doris Irving

A note from the editor

It has been a pleasure to work on this book with Doris Irving and her team – though sad too, for, like all the contributors to this book, I have lost a very good friend. This note is just to say that some of the writings here have been split among two or more sections; so if part of a contribution seems to be missing, you should find it in another section as you read on. Because some contributors wished to be anonymous, it seemed best simply to print a list of contributors at the back of the book.

Karen Johnson

1 By way of introduction

BCD with his great-nephew Benedict

A Tribute to Dr Brian Davies (given by Graham Benbow at the funeral)

Dear Family and Friends

We have come together today to mourn the passing and to pay our last respects to a truly incredible man, Dr Brian Collin Davies, a man who served this community and district for 32 years as its General Practitioner and Physician to the local hospital.

On behalf of the members of the Knighton Hospital and Community League of Friends and the Community and District in general I feel very honoured to be asked to convey this tribute. Each and every one of you, I know, will have your own thoughts and memories of what Dr Davies meant to you and which I know will remain with you for many years to come.

He was born in India in 1921 and returned to that country some 20 years later to serve as an officer in his beloved Gurkha Regiment. After the Second World War he returned to Oxford to train at medical college to become a General Practitioner. I am informed by good authority that all he ever wanted to be was a Rural General Practitioner.

BCD and his sister Barbara

And in the middle 50s he achieved his ambition by becoming a GP in my home town of Llanidloes, where as a young 14 year old boy I delivered milk to his house each morning.

It was at this time I recall, together with my parents and grandparents, being one of his patients until his departure to Knighton in July 1959. Llanidloes' loss was indeed Knighton's gain. The following year I came to live in Knighton myself and fortunately for me I became his patient again.

Dr Davies was someone we all envisaged as the traditional highly respected rural doctor, attending to patients and accident victims

2

anywhere, any time and in all kinds of weather. The condition of his cars were testimony to the speed at which he responded to emergency calls. A bashed door, a bumper hanging off or a wing rubbing on a wheel – and on one occasion not 100 yards from his surgery he demolished a wall belonging to the Horse and Jockey.

He also had a reputation for and was an expert in prescribing his own cures for minor ailments, among the most memorable being a cough linctus which he called his Swansea Medicine and also a special hand cream, both made up, of course, by the local pharmacist. And no doubt there are those among you who will remember his famous honey and black pepper mix for soothing a sore throat.

Dr Davies was not only a GP; he was also highly qualified in Midwifery, and this was an area of patient care he held very dear. Until local government reorganisation in 1974, as well as running his own practice he was also the medical officer of health for Knighton Urban District Council and the Knighton Rural District Council. He had wide-ranging responsibilities which included the quality of water supplies, sewage disposal, and the health of children in our schools.

BCD with his father and mother and sisters Barbara and Janet

Dr Davies at Llanidloes, 1955

There was no doubting the value he placed on retaining the community hospital when it was threatened with closure in the 1960s and the early 1970s. With others he led the protest campaigning against the Welsh Hospital Boards plans which resulted in a new hospital being built in Knighton. But he did not rest on his laurels. He carried forward his enthusiasm and with others founded the Hospital League of Friends in 1973 and for the last few years he has been our President.

He always displayed a great zest and enthusiasm for his profession which was second to none. Somehow he never appeared to be absent from work through illness and always appeared to be in a buoyant mood, frequently offering an appropriate quip and using, on occasions, a colourful and oft-times outrageous vocabulary. However, the confidence of his patients was absolute. The authority, knowledge and control of most situations were always the hallmark of Dr Davies' career for which, many of us in Knighton and District, will be eternally grateful.

A devotee of the concept of the National Health Service he argued vociferously for its preservation. Of the many reforms that have taken place over the last few years or so, there were some which he saw as a threat to the future of General Practice, as he had known it, but at the same time would concede were perhaps inevitable.

The contribution that Dr Davies has made to our hospital in partic-ular and the community in general will not be forgotten. In a fitting tribute in July 1991 the new Maternity Ward was opened and named The Brian Davies Ward with a plaque inscribed with gratitude for 32 years of dedicated service. And just recently the Knighton Town Council marked the communities' appreciation by proposing to name a new housing development in the town Davies Court. Knighton and District has indeed been honoured and blessed with the presence and devotion to duty of such an incredible man

To conclude this tribute to Dr Davies, I thought a few words in verse would help to express the love and gratitude we have all felt for him over many years:

> At all requests, you always came
> To help all those who ailed.
> If 'Day on Leave' or in the night
> You never ever failed.
>
> No matter weather, time or where,
> You got there just to serve.
> That love that goes with you today
> Is just what you deserve.
>
> A caring dedicated man
> Who loved his work so much.
> There are not many in this town
> Whose heart you did not touch.
>
> No other 'Doc' do we recall
> Who had such lasting zest.
> Please God, take care of this Great Man,
> The Best is now at Rest.

Dr Brian Davies (as read out by Dr John Ross at the funeral)

I became a physician at the Hereford Hospitals in 1961 and soon came to know Brian. I worked with him for the next 25 years. I rapidly realised what a remarkably fine doctor he was, and how lucky Knighton was to have him looking after families over a wide area and working at Knighton Hospital. Brian was very good at diagnosis and treatment, and his knowledge and care of his patients was outstanding. He did not work to time, as so many have to now – if someone needed extra time, they got it, and this was much appreciated. He visited patients at home at all times of day or night. If a patient needed admission to a Hereford Hospital at night, Brian would often avoid waiting for an ambulance and bring him or her to Hereford in his car. For many years he was without a partner in Knighton, and his hours of work must have been great.

He was a modest man and, usually, with humour. He liked to give the impression that he was a simple doctor working in a remote area. I once asked him if a patient we were discussing on the telephone had a temperature and he replied, 'We don't have clever instruments to measure things like that out here.'

In those days, we hospital doctors did many so-called domiciliary visits. A GP could ask a specialist to see a patient at home who was not ill enough to be admitted to hospital, but too ill to come to an outpatient clinic. It could be demanding after a day's work at the hospital but it was always a pleasure to be taken out into the country by Brian and to see how much he was liked and how much he knew about the patient and family. It was a bit of an adventure and even dangerous sometimes as Brian enjoyed taking short cuts across fields and the open countryside in his car.

He always had an interest in the history of medicine and built up a fine collection of old medical books. We in Hereford benefited from this, as he generously gave some books to our collection at the Hereford Postgraduate Centre and told us about those which he had noted were for sale.

I don't know much about his hospital work in Knighton except that his efforts to preserve the hospital and its maternity services were successful and widely admired. His retirement event in Knighton really did show us all how highly the town thought of him – a gathering of about 500 people, band playing and presentations including by the first baby and the last baby he had delivered.

When he retired, he attended a course in London on the history of medicine and subsequently gave a number of talks. It was impressive to see him speaking with a pile of his historical books in front of him, from which he quoted. Though living far from Hereford he had always been a regular attendant at lectures and social events at the Hereford Postgraduate Medical Centre, and he continued to come in retirement until he could no longer drive. We in Hereford do miss him and will remember him as a skilled and caring doctor and a very good friend.

Funeral address by Paul Clayden

Brian was my uncle by marriage. He met Alison, who was my mother's sister, when he was training to be a doctor at the Radcliffe Infirmary in Oxford where she was a ward sister. I first met Brian when he became engaged to Alison, in 1954 when I was thirteen. He came to our house in Henley-on-Thames with Alison, sporting a bow tie and smoking a cigarette in a long holder! My brother and I were ushers at their wedding in 1955. We visited them several times when they lived in Llanidloes.

When Brian and the family moved to Knighton it was not long before we were invited to visit. I remember that we spent the Christmas of 1962 there. Brian ordered us to leave on Boxing Day because of the likelihood of snow. How right he was – the very next day the snow fell and stayed on the ground until March. It was the worst winter in living memory.

After our marriage in 1964 (to which Alison and David came, but Brian could not leave the practice), Lyn and I and our three boys stayed with Brian and Alison on numerous occasions and always received the warmest of welcomes. We sometimes used to accompany Brian on his rounds. We became well attuned to his unique style of driving, which regarded obstacles and tight bends as challenges rather than hazards. On one occasion I allowed him to drive my car on a visit to the art gallery at Bleddfa. He swung the car into the wide drive but managed to scrape one of the gateposts! He was very contrite, but I was secretly amused – he was acting true to form!

Top: Brian and Alison Davies on their wedding day, 1955
Bottom left: Dr Davies with his father Cuthbert and his son David
Bottom right: BCD and family

Brian was an avid collector of books. He had a wonderful library, including many rare medical books relating to gynaecology, his special subject. We often used to go with him to the bookshops at Hay-on-Wye, in particular the Cinema Bookshop where Brian was an honoured customer, and to other local bookshops where he was well known. He generously supplied us with many children's books for our sons and more recently for our grandsons.

At one time, before the present surgery was built in the garden, Brian developed a passion for dahlias, in the cultivation of which he was greatly aided by his gardener Ted Morgan. He used a special ring to ensure that the blooms were the correct size to qualify for exhibiting at local shows. So keen was he that on one occasion he took Lyn into the garden at night to show her the best blooms by torchlight.

Brian had a large fund of stories and jokes which he always told me were passed on to him by patients. One story I particularly recall. Brian had certified the death of an elderly farm worker and the body was removed to the undertakers in Wylcwm Street. Shortly afterwards, he received an urgent call from the undertakers saying that noises were coming from a coffin and asked him to investigate. When the coffin was opened Brian was able to identify the noise as coming from a pacemaker which had not been removed from the body and was giving the signal that the battery needed replacing.

I sometimes asked Brian whether he would write his memoirs, but he always declined, saying that he would not be able afford the legal fees in defending himself against unjustified libel actions. I think this is a pity, because his experience as a country GP in an era of great change in the medical world would have been both valuable and interesting.

When Brian first arrived at Wylcwm Street, the surgery was a room in the main house (later turned into the library), with the waiting room next door (now a bathroom). As the practice grew, a new surgery was built on to the house and this was further expanded to its present size. If you want a permanent memorial to Brian's devotion to the health and well-being of the people of Knighton and the surrounding area, may I quote to you what is written on the tomb of Sir Christopher Wren in St. Paul's Cathedral: *si monumentum requiris, circumspice* (if you want a memorial, look around you).

After Alison's death in 1998, we continued to visit Brian regularly and kept in touch by telephone. The last time I spoke to him was on Boxing

Day 2008, a few days before his death. We had a good conversation, much of it about my mother, who was always close to both Alison and Brian. We all loved Brian very much and it was a great privilege to have known him for so much of our lives.

On the road through life, we meet some remarkable people, who make a difference to our lives. One of these was Dr Brian Davies. Often in the present Wylcwm Street Surgery, people in the waiting room will ask, 'Were you under Dr Davies?' They all want to express what a wonderful Doctor he was, to share memories. When I had my post office, ladies would come in and say, 'I've been under the Doctor'. Whatever did they mean? It always made me laugh. Dr Davies was known for his outrageous comments; he could be very naughty. He was a tonic, making one feel better, uplifted. He did not always approve of tonics, and would recommend a glass of stout.

Our family first met him over thirty years ago. We were told, make sure you sign on with Dr Davies. On a call to his surgery, he turned up at our home bringing with him the necessary medicine for our two children. He attended my aunt from Devon who had pneumonia. She never stopped talking about him. My mother-in-law, a very determined lady, opened up the water cap in her car when the engine boiled over. The water cascaded, scalding her arm and breast. She would let the first aid man look at her arm, but certainly look no further. She arrived with us late into the evening, and Dr Davies told her to smother the area with honey. It worked a treat. As beekeepers we would exchange honey remedies with him. He was known for his honey and pepper treatment of the throat.

It was always an experience to go to his old surgery, sometimes with queues outside the door. It was entertaining in the waiting room as there was much banter and chatter. You were sorry when your turn came round to go in to Dr Davies, as you would miss the end of an interesting story. How did he cope with so many patients? He always had time for each and everyone, and a kind word goes a long way.

Dr Davies was famous for his driving skills. His cars had rounded corners where he had hit walls, gates and other obstacles. He would get to places others couldn't reach, even in the depths of winter. Many a baby he delivered or he would be there for life's departures. He saw many spartan living conditions and the hardness of some lives.

Tribute must also be paid to Mrs Alison Davies. She was such a support to him, often helping people when he was out on call. She stitched up my husband, John's hand when he was bitten by a dog. It cannot be easy being a doctor's wife, as a big part of him belongs to his patients. He missed her greatly when she died, and we know he could be very lonely. So when retirement came to him, he did not find this easy. He would be seen many a morning sitting in his great friend Doris Irving's bookshop. He would be of help to her with book carrying etc. He would also be seen carrying his shopping basket, off to Prince and Pugh's for morning coffee. He would say, 'Sit down and have a coffee with me.' Here was a man who loved being amongst people.

Thinking back, now many years ago, he came to our village to see a lady who seemed always to be a little under the weather. He told her, 'You are a good woman going to waste.' She was not amused, but he was right. Her life had become one of drudgery with little outlet for herself to enjoy life. We must also remember not to be good people going to waste. We must use our talents and keep interests in life. He used to warn young ladies to beware of the Trouser fly!! He always jokingly commented that he could recognise people from their derrières – naughty naughty!

In a first aid box used in World War One, we found a glass phial of liquid. Dr Davies was intrigued by it. He said it was not medical, and he asked around, and no one came up with answers until a man came to do fire extinguishers. The liquid phial was to be thrown into buildings to cause an explosion, but very often, the one who was throwing it was at very great risk of being blown up. Dr Davies said he would like to keep it to display on his fireplace shelf. We have no idea to this day what he did with it. We just have to trust him!

He said he would not write a book about his experiences, he would leave that to others, but he was always encouraging me to write. He wrote in my autograph book in 2002:

> Be guarded in your relations with the ruling power , for those who exercise it draw no man near to them except in their own interests, and stand not by a man in his hour of need. (Words of Rabbi Gamaliel – a Pharisee teacher of the Apostle Paul. Described as tolerant and peaceful.) This advice still holds good.

Sir Thomas More was known as 'A Man for All Seasons'. Dr Brian Davies was surely 'A Man for All People'.

Our family had contact with Dr Davies over many years. In fact we were in early primary school when he came to be our GP in Knighton. He was a truly brilliant generalist, coping with midwifery, public health and clinical medicine, and an extremely competent, very hardworking general practitioner.

Not only was he an excellent doctor; he took such interest in us as a family. He was particularly supportive when our father died aged 50 when we were but teenagers. Equally, many years later he personally drove our step-father to Bronllys when he needed hospital admission.

He encouraged both Trevor and Barry to go to university and Barry particularly, despite coming from a non-medical family, to train as a doctor. Whenever Barry went to see Dr Davies when he was at home during holidays, he always had an amusing story to tell. Dr Davies also followed Sue's career with great interest as she trained as a nurse and then midwife. When she eventually went as a medical missionary to the Congo he sent journals to keep her up to date.

However, perhaps the lasting memory Sue will have of Dr Davies is about two years ago when he was making one of his many trips up Broad Street towards Prince and Pugh's shop, carrying his shopping basket. He saw her and in his usual way said, 'Girl, come and have a cup of tea with me.' Sue was busy shopping at the time, but knowing how he had always had time for people she accepted his offer and was treated to a mid-morning drink. During that time he asked about all of us and what we were doing, including teasing Sue that at last a man had been courageous enough to marry her!

Our family feel a deep sense of gratitude towards him. He was dedicated to his job and never seemed to be really off duty – Knighton was indeed privileged to have such a superb GP for so many years.

My first encounter with Brian Davies was in November 1970. My parents had been separated for some years, my father having gone to live and work in America. Then in the spring of that year my mother announced, 'Your father and I are going to live together again.'

'Is that wise?' I asked.

'Oh, yes,' replied my mother. 'We are both in our seventies now.'

And so it became necessary to find a house large enough for us all, and my mother found the Old Rectory at Bleddfa, which I bought for my parents that August when my father came back from the States and moved in. In no time at all the old drinking and rows began, and in November my mother had a mild heart attack and I sent for our local doctor from Knighton, Dr Brian Davies. After examining my mother he took me on one side and said bluntly, 'There's only one thing wrong with your mother: it's your father!' Over the years I came to appreciate this directness of his, never hesitating to call a spade a spade, though there were those who could never get used to it!

As a GP he was the last of his kind. The stories are countless of how he would turn up at any hour of the night or day to some remote farm-house in the hills to deliver a baby, or tend a dying or a dead person. He might be at a lecture in the evening in Hereford and, receiving a telephone call, would at once drive to wherever the patient was. Many hundreds can testify to his devotion to his work, the kind of personal doctoring that now belongs to another era and a different ethos. Once when we went for a drive over the hills and stopped for tea in a cafe in Llanidloes, a woman got up from an adjoining table and came across, saying, 'It is Dr Davies, isn't it? You won't remember me, but you brought me into the world!'

He and his wife Alison first met in Oxford when he was a junior doctor and she was a Sister on the Paediatric Ward at the Radcliffe Hospital. After the birth of their only son, she suffered intermittently from post natal depression and at intervals had to be admitted to Talgarth. He would drive over the hills to visit her and on his way back, dispirited by these visits, he would stop off at the little church at Rhulen, in the hills between Hay and Painscastle. Although he was, and remained, an agnostic, he found great peace there which he told me on more than one occasion. There is no doubt that after the death of Alison he experienced great loneliness. They had both been great readers and of an evening would sit either side of the fire, each engrossed in a book. After her death there were occasions, he told me, when he would look up from his book and 'see' Alison on the other side of the fireplace, reading. But always he pooh-poohed any idea of the paranormal.

After he retired he would often talk about his early experiences as a young doctor. Once speaking about having to give lumbar injections to small children and their screams, his whole body suddenly shook with the memory that had been repressed all those years and he began to weep. On another occasion it was recalling his having to deal with the fatal accident of an undergraduate who, attempting to climb a spire, had fallen and crushed his skull. Again the tears flowed. One began to realise what terrible things any doctor has to witness and yet, while in practice, detach himself from their emotional impact.

During his retirement he proved a great help to Doris Irving at the Bookshop in Knighton, doing the school deliveries for her, and each day he would help check the parcels of new orders as they came in. He also involved himself with the Bleddfa Centre and its work. The Bleddfa Trust owes him a great debt. Not only was he was associated with it from early on but after the death of Alison it became like a second home to him. At gallery openings he loved to don an apron and rubber gloves and help Elizabeth Reynolds and others in the kitchen wash up, often trying to shock them with ribald remarks! He gave hundreds of books to the Centre to be sold, and regularly bought from the gallery and the shop. He more than once said to me, 'I would hate to see that place go under.'

After his retirement and until he had to give up driving, he and I had an arrangement that whenever I had to go up to London by train, or return, he would meet me in his car, and I would hand him a cheque for his favourite charity, the Friends of Knighton Hospital, for which he had worked so hard. Just towards the end he would occasionally shoot through a red light, and I recall one of the nurses at the hospital, when I told her that Dr Brian Davies used to drive me to the station, replying, 'Oh, you are brave!' Always I used to thank him and always he would reply, 'What else are we here for but to help one another?' His whole philosophy was summed up in those few words.

So many people will have their own memories of him which if they were all woven together would make a patchwork quilt of many colours. He touched so many lives, both their beginnings and their endings, while his countless unsung acts of kindness and generosity will continue to send up green shoots in the lives of those of us who were fortunate enough to know him, whether as our doctor or as our friend.

I believe I was his first holiday locum in 1970. He had me over for a day to check me over and we saw over 50 patients in the surgery, Knighton Hospital, Llandrindod Hospital and at the patient's home – this was all done at his customary pace!

He still telephoned me regularly during his holiday to check what sort of a job I was doing, and importantly to guide me through the various characters and their behaviour, which he knew so well. The latter was so much part of a traditional Family Doctor – continuity for years.

In 1967 when I was a junior doctor in Hereford, I remember he arrived in casualty in the night with a very ill patient in his car – a decision he would make from time to time, bearing in mind the long distance to Hereford and not delaying for the arrival of an ambulance to an isolated house. This was a calculated move which I also used to do, following his example, during my 30 years of general practice in this area. (This was not without anxiety –the doctor's, I mean!)

I was particularly struck by his affection and respect for his involve-ment with the Gurkhas. Many people may not have known much about his wartime experiences, which had a profound effect on him. I cannot put into words what he told me. Like many who survived, he had to start his career after losing his youth in fighting for freedom.

He was a man of many interests, particularly people – he was a natural NHS doctor and would not entertain private practice.

He was sensitive to Alison's difficulties – and both showed us all how to cope. Perhaps Brian threw himself into his work more as a result. They had many friends locally who were only too pleased to support them.

He could identify unsavoury personalities for whom he had a special description – a Snerd. I cannot translate that for you! He was a real man – kind, but not wet with it. He would stick with his patients until the end. My sort of hero.

My first encounter with Dr Davies was after having written to him asking if he needed help when his new surgery was built. I had had experience in Medical Records, and also South Metropolitan Cancer Registry, and locumed when asked at Lambeth Hospital Radiotherapy Dept. with Dr Parfitt (who said he would give me a reference). I got a phone call saying, 'Can you come down on Saturday afternoon? Then we can have a talk.'

Arriving in Knighton early, I went up the Narrows to Browns the Bakers. As I stepped out, a Land Rover tore down the street and nearly squashed me flat. I said, 'Oh darn', or something like that, and shook my fist at the driver.

I knocked on the doctor's side door and as you have guessed, there stood the Land Rover driver. We both collapsed laughing and he put the kettle on. I found that my reference from Dr Parfitt was really glowing: 'She laughs a lot and lets you have a chocolate biscuit.' I mean, nothing about, 'She can spell rhabdomyosarcoma'!

Scene: Drinking tea and doing the post. Phone rings. Loud voice of a woman. 'Come quick, she's bulling.' 'Will come as soon as you've got a nail on the door to hang my coat on.' Short silence. Voice: 'Is that the AI man?' 'No, Dr Davies, but feel free, girl.' The Doc then gave her the AI man's number.

Scene: New surgery, warm summer afternoon. Doc was having work done in the house and the front door was wide open. John, Doc's younger son, appeared at Reception. 'Mrs Irving, a man has been watching cricket in the front room with me and I think he really wants to see Dad.' I went to the front room to find an elderly gent, and asked him if he wanted to see Dr Davies. 'My,' said he, 'He must be busy. I've been watching cricket for half an hour, and I only need a cuppa.' I pointed out the new surgery and new waiting room, and then made him his cuppa.

Scene. Surgery. Having typed up the morning reports, I felt I had to query one dictation (tape recorded). Dr D was referring to a grizzled old farmer who was a favourite of us both. He had had a carpal tunnel operation on his hand and was reported as saying that the operation was in his opinion not efficacious. The eff bit fitted OK, but I asked, 'Did he really say that?' 'No,' says Doc. He said, 'Well Doc, to my mind it wasn't worth a shit.' 'OK', says I, 'Near enough.'

Doc D asked me, 'Would you like to come out on the rounds to see where the patients live?' This was before mobile phones and in emergency I could ask someone to go out on the road and stop him. We went in the dreaded Land Rover and raced all round Llangunllo and Llanbister,

15

delivering prescriptions and good cheer. On returning, he said, 'Just in case, girl, how about you parking the Land Rover?' That meant backing into the yard and tight reversing into the garage. He got out, and God was kind and I reversed smoothly into the garage. Boy, was he peeved. Not a bump or scratch. (Still don't know how I did it – probably God does.)

Rob and I went away for a weekend to a friend's wedding and left Dad with the two dogs. Whilst we were away our dear old terrier Wally died from a heart attack, and Dad didn't tell us, so as not to spoil our trip. We discovered that Lyn Lewis, the Vet and Dr D had buried Wally in Dr D's garden with a little bit of ceremony, as my Dad was heartbroken.

In 1983 in Dad's last illness he couldn't have had kinder treatment. Every night the Doc came to give the painkilling injection, then sat on the bed with a cup of tea till Dad dropped off to sleep. This was much appreciated by us.

I have fond memories of Alison Davies. We laughed a lot and shared a common interest in Early English music. When Brian retired, they lunched with us and joined our visiting friends. Our friends were their friends. After Alison's death, Brian joined Rob, myself and our friend Gladys Lewis in many holidays. We self catered because of dogs. Brian washed up and became adept at the morning poo patrol. He said he had found his niche. We made him watch Coronation Street, accompanied by his mutterings, but had a lot of laughs as well.

BCD and Robert Irving on holiday

When Brian's 80th birthday was coming up, Rob and I decided to hold a giant tea party for him We could only have under 50 invitations, as space and weather were considerations. A request on the invitation was *secrecy*, and not a word got out. At the family lunch on the Saturday Rob casually invited Brian to tea along with Jan and Mike the next day, as after the Saturday things would be a bit flat. OK, he said. 3.30, says I. By kind permission of Mrs Susan Hailes all cars were to be parked away out of sight. Rob was directing at the gate, and Brian Whittle and Brian

Above: Brian cuts his cake at his 80th birthday party
Below: Rob, Doris and Brian at the party

Thomas did carpark duties. Friends did refreshments and Ruth Davies obtained several card tables to put in the stable yard. A phone call from Jan, and we hid all our guests. As Brian drove in his face was a picture, and his language was fruity. When it came to cutting his cake, made and iced by mother and daughter patients, he was really choked. Tea was served to 48 visitors, and a lot of chat accompanied same.

One evening, when being treated to a lovely supper at the Riverside Inn with Brian, Jan and Mike, and Rob, I went to the counter as Brian was not at his best that day and was a bit muddled. As we were sorting the bill out, a man came up to the counter and asked if he was Dr Davies. Brian agreed that he was, and to his surprise and my delight the chap said, 'Twenty years ago in the snow my doctor couldn't come and we rang you, and you came immediately to see my son, who by then was very ill. You put him into your car with his mother and took him to Hereford, and we never got to thank you as we were distraught and moved house soon after. Please may I shake your hand and bless you.' The faces of the other customers were a study.

My last happy memory of Brian Davies, whom I felt privileged to call a friend, was Christmas Day 2008. He came as usual with his carer,

Dr Davies and his sister Jan, 16 December 2008

Christmas Day 2008

Michael. We had a friend from Bucknell and one from Wakefield. We had our meal, watched the Queen's Speech, opened our presents and had a good chat and laugh.

I could see he was tiring, and he was also lumbered with one of our cats for at least an hour, until his carer at last made a move for home. As I saw them out, Brian gave me a hug and said, 'Girl, I've had a smashing day.' When sitting at his bedside in Llandrindod Hospital I remembered this, and felt that a good and eventful life had at last come to an end. God bless him.

'It's OK, I'm on my way'

2 Army days

Doctor Brian Collin Davies - obituary in *The Sirmoree*, Summer 2009

Major Brian Davies, who died on 2nd January 2009 at the age of 87, was the last surviving officer of the Regiment to have commanded a company of the 4th Battalion in Burma during the Second World War. He was a very good soldier and a cheerful and friendly man who throughout his life, in his own words to the author, thought 'I have been bloody lucky and am grateful'.

Brian was born on 14 July 1921. His father had served in the 1st Gurkha Rifles in France during the First World War, in the 3rd Afghan War of 1919 and the Waziristan Campaign, and afterwards became Reader in Indian History at Oxford University. Brian was sent to Merchant Taylors' School in London, and left it to enlist in The Welch Fusiliers at the age of 18. In March 1941 he was commissioned into The Welch Regiment and volunteered for the Indian Army. He sailed for India in April 1942 and was sent to the 5th Battalion 1st Gurkha Rifles, then newly raised at Dharmsala.

In August 1943 Brian was transferred to the 2nd Goorkhas and joined the 4th Battalion with which he served at first on the North West Frontier in Damdil and Razmak as Station Staff Officer at Damdil and Battalion Transport Officer. Before the battalion moved to Rawalpindi he

was given command of A Company which he then led until he left the Regiment after the war. The 4th Battalion went to Burma in March 1945 where he and his company almost immediately carried out a long range penetration patrol to Toyokkon, and captured Myingung on the Irrawaddy. They also played a prominent part in the Battle of Tanbingon on 2nd July 1945 for which Major Peter Collins, who was killed there, was recommended for the Victoria Cross and Brian for an immediate Military Cross. Neither was awarded, both being mentioned in despatches instead.

Once the war was over, Brian left the battalion at Tharawaddy in September, for home and demobilization. In 1946

Brian Davies and his father, Cuthbert Davies

he went to Balliol College, Oxford, to read Medicine and qualified as a doctor in 1953. Thereafter, in turn, he was a Medical Officer at Knighton Hospital, Radnor, a House Surgeon at the Radcliffe Infirmary, Oxford, and Obstetrician and House Surgeon at Dudley Road Hospital, Birmingham. Then, [after a spell in general practice in Llanidloes], he decided to go into National Health Service General Practice in Knighton, where he worked until he retired on his 70th birthday.

Brian was such a keen member of The Sirmoor Club from its very beginning (as the Regimental Association) until he died that it is a great pity he lived too far away to attend our reunions without great difficulty. We are lucky, though, to have his reminiscences of the war, which were published in *The Sirmooree* [reproduced below]. We send our deepest sympathy to his two sons.

Dr Brian Davies reminisces (from *The Sirmooree*, Winter 1996/97:

I joined the 4/2 GR at Damdil (Indian North West Frontier) in the late summer of 1943. Damdil was then a two battalion camp on the Central Waziristan Road about half way between Bannu, which was inside the administrative border, and Razmak camp, some 77 miles into Tribal Territory and about 6,500 feet above sea level. Damdil was, if I remember rightly, something over 4,000 feet and was still a malarial area. There were then no drugs for anti-malarial prophylaxis and strict rules were in force about the use of mosquito nets and long clothes after dark. The camp served to house troops whose main duty was to protect traffic using the road on Road Open Days. Garrisons along the road and at Razmak provided a deterrent to local tribal hotheads and a threat to their villages. In these duties we were aided by the Tochi Scouts who manned various small forts in the area and worked in close co-operation with the Political Agents. I once spent two weeks on attachment to the Scouts which taught me a lot and left me with a profound admiration for them and for their British Officers, who worked under conditions of great hardship and isolation.

The Political people had a very important say in what went on and were very anxious to avoid any action by the military which might inflame the local tribes. At that time this was even more important as demands on the major theatres of war involving Germans or Japanese meant that there were no reserves which could be brought in should more serious trouble arise on the Frontier - trouble which could spread rapidly to involve relatively large numbers of troops and out of which little lasting benefit would come. Our involvement in three Afghan Wars had brought this home to us; a bitter lesson which the Russians were later to learn.

Apart from the 'Road Open Days' life was reasonably quiet. Outlying pickets had to be manned and relieved and some patrol work was done. My first job was to be Station Staff Officer. No one seemed able to tell me what this entailed except the duty clerk. One's duty was to check station stores. This was more urgent than usual because it appeared that there was a deficit in latrine pans and, more seriously still, there were seven medium machine guns and 14,000 rounds of ammunition missing. I had to get busy. Eventually it turned out that all these items were safely in the camp or the outlying pickets. What had happened was that, some time before, a slack regiment had, on leaving and unsupervised by Brigade, not bothered with a check of outlying pickets but had a list of what lay immediately to hand and passed this off as a true inventory to the incoming battalion. Brigade had been slack too. Shortly after this I was made Transport Officer. On pointing out respectfully that I had neither driving licence nor mechanical experience, I was told that we had 37 vehicles in the unit and I had better take one and find out – ideal advice in a perimeter camp on a mountain road in hostile territory.

Some weeks later we were moved up to Razmak and were put to more risky road protection duties. Razmak Brigade were responsible for covering the road from the camp itself up to the Razmak Narai, which was a pass some miles up the road and about 7,500 feet above sea level. (Narai means a pass in Pushtu.) The Narai was overlooked by Alexandra Picket on the adjacent spur at about 8,000 feet. It consisted of a 'Beau Geste' type fort held by a company garrison which was changed over once a month. It was said to be the highest permanently manned post in the British Empire. A lonely month for the company commander, who saw the rest of his regiment only on 'Road Open Days'. The Razmak sector of the road was overlooked by much larger hills than we had been used to at Damdil. Large areas were rocky and steep hillsides with dense scrub and gave splendid cover for the guerrilla strikes at which the local Wazir and Mahsud tribes were past masters.

This was brought home to us savagely one day when we went out on a training scheme which, unfortunately, took too much account of the 'story' behind the scheme and not enough of the local terrain and tribesmen. The locals came in through the scrub and broken ground between us and the camp. We lost 30 men killed and were ordered to cut our losses and get back to camp as best we could. A neighbouring battalion who were ordered out to cover our retreat lost several men and one of their company commanders. The Politicals told us later that there had been upwards of a thousand tribesmen in contact with us that night. One of our company commanders, Norman Lockey, was awarded the MC for his work.

In winter Razmak was bitterly cold. Outlying pickets and posts on the perimeter wall had braziers or wood stoves at night and wore Poshteen coats of sheepskin, balaclavas and Gilgit boots. These latter were thigh length boots of quilted felt with leather soles. They needed all this. Firewood for the camp was brought in by locals on camels or donkeys and arranged in a huge stack at the lower end of the camp. This gave rise to a serio-comic outbreak of VD for which the medicals were unable to account. They eventually traced it to the firewood stack, which the enterprising locals had constructed hollow with small 'cubicles' and had imported women dressed as camel boys.

That winter we were given four armoured carriers; wheeled type from the desert. These were gun quads turned back to front and armoured. They had stood in the open during the monsoon and we were to wait a further six months for the essential tools for them. I was sent with the vehicles and some men down to Mari Indus and told to train up drivers and driver/mechanics; no tools and me still waiting for an MT course. Fortunately we had attached a splendid cockney Sergeant who kept us roadworthy and we got some men trained. Mari Indus was a fascinating place where the Indus debouches from the hills onto the plains. The main railway stopped there and a metre gauge line crossed the river on a splendid bridge and went on up to the Frontier base stations at Bannu and Dera Ismail Khan, taking nearly all day on the journey. When the little train crossed the bridge there was a shower of four anna pieces which the men threw into the river to ensure a return trip. In summer the train earned its nickname of the 'Heatstroke Express'. It stopped midday at Lakki Marwat for lunch, which was invariably duck curry with tinned pears and caramel custard to follow. Officers travelling in the hot weather used to club together to buy a large block of ice which was supposed to

Christmas Day 1943, showing BCD and Norman Lockey with their fellow soldiers in the Gurkha Regiment (photographs kindly lent by Mrs Lockey)

keep the compartment cool. At Mari Indus and in the neighbouring Salt Range there were deposits of rock salt which were mined and sent on down the river on boats made on the river bank, the timber for which came down as huge logs floated from the forests far to the north.

During the summer of 1944 I was sent from Razmak to Calcutta to do a course in fire fighting. The course instruction was based on a good water supply from the mains. None of it would have been applicable to our situation on the frontier and even less to conditions in Burma in the monsoon. Probably it had been decided that every station above a certain size should have an office trained in fire fighting. From Calcutta the next stop was Arangaon near Poona for the long awaited MT course. This proved most useful to me later on in civilian life but was little use at the time as on return to the 4/2 my job was changed to 'A' Company Commander, relying largely on mules. I am always grateful that I was never sent away on a mule course. The best bit of the MT course was learning to waterproof Jeeps and trucks for wading ashore from landing craft. We then had to drive the vehicle through six foot of water for a quarter of a mile circuit. Had the job not been properly done and water got in, there was just no way that you could bull-shit your way out of it – a rare condition in army training.

The battalion then moved down to near Rawalpindi for training in less restricted conditioned and for toughening up for long distance marching preparatory to going into Burma. As we had no jungle experience, two companies were sent down to the thickly forested area west of Bangalore City and under the Nilgiri Hills. This was a fascinating exercise and gave us greatly needed confidence in navigating on a compass bearing in thick country. Eventually we found ourselves on the way to the real war. We went by train across India and then by lorry over to Imphal. From there the battalion came on by road while two company commanders were flown on down to the Irrawaddy to be attached to a battle hardened and well respected unit, the 4/10 GR. They were nicknamed the 'Nonstop Gurkhas'. One happy memory of the road to Imphal – at one point we were ordered to break bulk and each man was to carry his own rations. A sizeable amount of this was raspberry jam in ten pound tins. I have a mental picture of a long file of Gurkha Riflemen in full battle order moving past me with each man holding on (not in) his right hand a big piece of a banana leaf surmounted by a huge lump of raspberry jam. They loved the taste. We company commanders travelled by Dakota down to a landing strip just north of the Irrawaddy which we were to cross at the 2 Corps ferry.

Our Jeep was okay apart from having no brakes. This presented a problem when we got on the ferry as I was made to back off until my rear wheels were on the edge of the pontoon to try to counterbalance the weight of a 'Sherman' tank up front. I clung desperately to the side girders of the pontoon and hoped that the river was not as wide as it looked or as fast flowing. All went well and we caught up with 4/10 GR, who turned out to be kindly and wonderful tutors. The company to whom I was attached were sent, riding on tanks, in a quick dash across country to cut the Rangoon to Mandalay road. It was the dry season and the tanks kicked up a fearsome lot of dust. On arriving on the road we found that we had captured some sort of advanced medical post. The staff had decamped after, so the locals told us, shooting all the wounded who could not move. The rest tried to hide in the bushes where most of them blew themselves up on grenades. Two Japanese actually came in and surrendered to our company commander. They stank to high heaven and were a mass of maggots on large areas of bad burns. Not knowing any better, we cleaned the maggots off and passed them back, with clean dressings, for our medicals and intelligence to deal with. They told us that they had both been in Hong Kong as businessmen and did not believe their army propaganda that we would torture and kill all prisoners. I hope they got home safely.

Soon after this 4/2 GR arrived and I rejoined my own company. We were now part of 20 Indian Division. Our people were getting ready to deal with the Japanese in the oil fields and in Meiktila. 20 divisions were to go on south below the oil fields and then to swing west towards the river. It was known that a lot of boats were being collected near the oil fields presumably to get away down river. To frustrate this a detachment called Dave Force with me in command was sent on to the river bank.

We were 'A' Company 4/2 GR; one company of Deception Force under a crazy-brave and splendid chap called Flash Alf Richardson, some 3" mortars and two armoured cars. Our job was to destroy boats coming downstream which we did with reasonable success until the rest of 4/2 GR were moved up. While we were engaged in this one of our attached Jeep Ambulance drivers came to me in great distress. He was one of the American Field Service drivers – men whose devotion and bravery were legendary in Burma. He wanted a doctor which we hadn't got. If we had no doc, then a syringe and needle would do. Why? Well, Herman was very bad and likely to die so I went to see Herman thinking that he was another driver. I found that Herman was a baby owl who had been blown out of his nest by a nearby shell burst. The ambulance man was making an attempt to rear Herman on a diet of rice porridge which was served up in a lid of a round fifty cigarette tin. The poor owl was to perch on the edge of this and had his head pushed down into the mess. I don't think owls feed this way. Herman just got his beak and nostrils clogged; he must have died, I suppose.

When the rest of the battalion arrived it was decided that, as a surprise move, 'A' Company should go down river by boat lightly equipped and wearing plimsolls – our heavy packs and boots to come on in a bigger boat behind us. On the evidence of our experience of the vulnerability of men in boats, I said that it would be most unwise but was told to shut up and get on with it. This we did, leaving in the darkness of the early hours. Mercifully no one took any notice of us. We kept getting stuck on sandbanks but struggled (more truly straggled) down river until dawn when we went ashore. The bigger boat with our equipment got badly stuck (on purpose?) and all our blankets were stolen. Luckily we got our boots back after some days as our plimsolls were breaking up rapidly. We pushed on downstream with the rest of the battalion a short way behind.

All the villages were empty of Japanese and some had been torched. It was thirsty work and our first objective in any village was the well. Invariably this had been defiled by human excrement before the Japanese had pulled out. In addition to which, after 'pleasuring themselves' on the local women, they had thrown the used condoms down the well where they floated among the turds like obscene water lilies. Fortunately we were following the river but the banks were usually high and sheer making access to the water almost impracticable until we came to a bay where the banks dropped to water level. Here we thought was access but the bay was full of a log jam of timber, or so we thought at first. On closer inspection the logs turned out to be bodies of Japanese soldiers caught in an eddy. That seemed to be that, but the men were not so easily frustrated. Some long bamboos were cut down and used to urge our floaters into the main stream. The current was given fifteen minutes to scour out the bay and we were able to refill water bottles and to chlorinate them from the concentrate bottle carried by one man in each section. Some way further down the river we came to a large thickly wooded hill shaped like a pudding basin upside down and sporting a large 'Pagoda' on its top. This was Mount Popa. It was sacred to the Hamadryad or King Cobra and reputed to be swarming with the reptiles. It was also reported to have enemy in position on it. 'A' Company was told to attack it at first light, to the horror of its company commander. Mercifully this order was countermanded during the night.

A few days later, and still pushing south, the battalion was being led by 'C' Company under their Subedar, the company Major having lost an eye and been evacuated. A wireless message came back from 'C' Company for a British Officer to go up urgently. They had captured a man, the like of whom they had never seen before but as the only word he said that they recognised was 'F ...' they assumed that he was a British Officer! I went forward and was amazed to find sitting on a local pony, with only a head rope to control it, a most unusual man. He had a leonine head of hair with a full beard and moustache of ginger hue on top of which was a maroon paratroop beret. His shirt was khaki with a captain's pips and parachute wings, his lower half being clad in a red and green loincloth and heavy ammunition boots. He carried an American carbine and a native bag of hand grenades. His language was as reported. I think that, being new to the area, he had mistaken our men for Japanese. It turned out that he was one of a three man group from Force 136 and a very good chap he turned out to be. We saw a lot of his group in the subsequent weeks. Since the war I have come across his name on the learned government guidebooks at Tintern Abbey and Cilgerran Castle.

Our next move was eastwards towards the Pegu Yoma hills. We had to walk up the road going east from the Okpo crossroads which was 114 miles from Rangoon on the road to Prome. On three occasions we had to attack the village of Tanbigon to drive out Japanese units which had taken possession. On the third of these actions we lost Peter Collins, a very brave officer. Not long after this we were pulled in to rest and retrain for the recapture of Malaya. We were quartered in the Police Barracks at Tharrawaddy in the other half of which was one of the Frontier Force battalions. One night I was woken by an awful yelling and other noise from the FF lines. All I could see was a big bonfire surrounded by dancing Sikhs clad only in scarlet underpants and with their hair flying loose. It was a worrying sight until, on a balcony, appeared a group of their officers waving bottles and shouting encouragement to their men. So I went back to bed. Next morning we were told that the war was over.

3 The good doctor

BCD with Jo Mayall, Matron at Knighton Hospital

Dr Davies was in every way a country GP. He loved the rural life, and his experiences of army life with the Gurkha Regiment had prepared him well for any hardships, and helped with his ability to handle the foibles and occasional eccentric characteristics of some of his patients!

He was my parents' GP and we well remember his prompt action when called, and his help during their final illnesses. In modern parlance he was a 'twenty four seven' worker, with weather being no deterrent. He seemed almost to relish navigating through blizzards and the odd snow drift was no threat, as like most things in his life he took them head on!

In the late 1950s we had a contract to supply cars from the Milebrook Garage to operate what was known as 'The Sitting Case Car Service'. This was a way of transporting patients to Hospital Departments, Eye Clinics, Physiotherapy Departments etc. for all kinds of different treatments, including transporting disabled men into the Cheshire Home for respite care. This allowed the ambulance services to be free to attend more serious cases.

The Doctor would ring to request a car and driver without disclosing too much of the case history. The conversation once went along the lines of, 'Got a case for you, girl. Could you take this one, a poorly girl needing some T.L.C. Talk to her.'

'What should I talk about Doctor?' I asked.

'Oh anything – clothes, make up, you'll think of something, knowing you, but just go easy on the boyfriends.'

So without realising it, we had become untrained counsellors!

I well remember the Doctor's mirth when we had to report a driver taking an expectant mother to Copthorne Hospital, holding a torch for a midwife to deliver her baby on the Church Stretton bypass! It was a marvellous service as we got to know what the Doctor wanted and he had the confidence in us to get it right – or else!

His driving was well known, with the car easy to recognize by the many dents or bits hanging off. We heard of him racing up the Teme Valley and 'ditching' a very staid retired Matron who asked in her most sarcastic tone, 'Doctor, was it a serious heart attack or a haemorrhage that you were racing to?'

'No, girl,' came the reply, 'just a bit of fishing.'

On hearing of the loss of his late wife Alison, I wrote a short note mentioning the times we had had such fun in the Tref-y-Clawdd Women's

Institute and how she had loved to party. I realized how painful it must have been for him with his professional knowledge, watching Alison as the illness worsened.

Dr Davies was a unique person. His energies were boundless, whatever the cause. We shall always remember him in his retirement as he went up and down the Knighton streets with a basket on one arm and the other stretched out behind.

This is but a snap shot of the busy life of a lovable country GP who became everyone's friend. When the memoirs of his life are complete, it would surely be appropriate for every modern surgery's bookshelf to contain a version, as a reminder of days gone by. Now that would be a fitting testimony to a wonderful doctor's life.

Dr Davies was just as conscientious in his care for visitors as for his regular patients. My father was over from the Midlands putting in the wiring for the new bungalow we were building. That night I woke up for some reason, and as I lay awake I heard someone get up to go to the bathroom. This was followed by a thud. I shot out of bed and rushed to the bathroom to find my father collapsed on the floor. I shouted to my husband that I was going to fetch Doc Davies. We had a car but no phone so I raced from Rockes Meadow to Wylcwm Street and rang the bell. About five seconds later a head appeared from a bedroom window. At the word 'collapsed' the head had disappeared but a voice shouted, 'I'm on my way.' He arrived back at our home almost the same time as I did, pyjamas under the trousers, as was his wont.

The Doc examined my dad and said he was fine. All he needed to remember was not to get out of bed too quickly, and to pee slowly! However, the Doc was there the next day just to see how my dad was.

At three months old, Lesley had bronchial pneumonia and had to go to hospital. As a result of the medication she had a bleeding stomach ulcer, and she cried a lot, though we were told not to let her cry. After lots of sleepless nights, one night neither of us could console her and at 2am we called Dr Davies, who came within minutes. By this time Lesley was beginning to calm down. Peter and I were exhausted. Dr Davies looked at us and said, ' You to go to bed. I'll stay with Lesley until she goes back to sleep,' so we did. About half an hour later we heard him coming upstairs to he put Lesley into her cot. He poked his head around the door said goodnight and let himself out. He had probably been out on calls every night himself.

We were spending a weekend in Knighton in June 1972 looking at the schools, property and areas of interest; the sorts of things you do when you have a couple of kids aged nine and seven, and are thinking of moving. We had come up from Berkshire, having been offered a job at Motorway Remoulds.

On the Sunday afternoon we all ended up at the Dorcas Offices in what is now the completed Rockes Meadow Estate, but was then largely meadow land with only a few properties here and there. The boys were playing happily outside in the sunshine whilst we looked at the various plans. Suddenly, we heard lots of screaming and shouts, of 'Mum,' and 'Dad, please come quick.'

We all rushed outside to discover that whilst playing along one of the hedgerows, the boys had disturbed a wasps' nest and had already been stung many times. Ben Kemish quickly said, 'You want the Doc,' and promptly rang him up and explained the situation over the phone.

'Send them round to me,' was Brian's instant reply.

I asked Ben where we would find the surgery and he started to explain and spell Wylcwm Street to me, but that as it was a one way street, we would have to go around by the Clock Tower.

'Don't worry about the No Entry sign, just tell him to turn right by the Norton then take the first left,' said Brian, 'and I'll be waiting by The Horse & Jockey!'

We did as instructed, and after the Doc had seen to the boys and given them drinks and sweets, Carole had met Alison and things were nearly back to normal, he turned to me – a complete stranger until about 15 minutes earlier – and said, 'What do you know about crabs?'

In my innocence I assumed he was talking about crabs that live in the sea, so my reply was along the lines of, 'I didn't realise we were that close to the coast here in Knighton.' He did a sort of snort then said, 'Come and take a look at these fine specimens under the microscope. It's amazing what some long distance drivers can bring home!'

I am here today because of Dr Davies. Many years ago I was shopping in Burtons when I was stung by a wasp, which was crawling in my hair. Normally this wouldn't have bothered me, but on this occasion the sting went into a vein, travelled up my left arm and stopped my heart.

I knew nothing of what followed until later. Apparently Doc Davies threw me on the floor and lifted my legs up, which started my heart again. When I came to I found myself lying on a stone floor and wondering what I was doing there!

The only slightly funny thing that happened was that Doc Davies ,having promised my mother a lift, drove off leaving her standing, and drove up the Ffrydd from where we'd moved six months before!

I must have looked pretty awful as apparently I turned blue and at least one child had to go to the doctor after seeing me!

So you can see how much I owe to Doc Davies, along with countless others. He was irreplaceable.

Whilst we were in hospital awaiting the birth of our second child, our eight year old was rushed into the same hospital with a convulsion. Not only did the Doc carry him out to the ambulance; he also took the time to write me a long letter in which he explained why he had seen the need to hospitalise him and assured me he would be fine. Thank goodness he was.

My husband cut the top third of his thumb off whilst working on his car. It lay in his palm joined only by a piece of skin. I phoned the Doc and explained what had happened and that he would be coming straight up to the surgery. It was 8am. When he arrived, the Doc had some foaming liquid in a bowl and said, 'Put it in there, boy,' to which my husband replied, 'But it will drop off!' 'Don't worry,' was the reply. 'We'll find it in the bottom!' He put 3 stitches in the thumb, bound it up and told him to keep sniffing it. As long as it didn't smell it would be OK. It was, and he still has it.

We were in Scotland on holiday. I had been having severe lower cramp pains and had to be taken to hospital. They could not find out what was the matter. I had already had several bouts at home over the past 6 months and Dr Davies had treated me. Peter suggested the doctor rang to find out how I had been treated at home, as I was nearly unconscious with the pain. After I had been treated and could converse, the doctor asked me if I was a personal friend of Dr Davies. I said only as a patient and asked why. It turned out that when he rang Dr Davies and told him my name, Dr Davies immediately told him what was wrong with me, and how he treated me. The Scottish doctor was really impressed and commented that Dr Davies didn't have to get my records out to look up how I had been treated. He said he must be a remarkable man, which we all know he was.

It is not surprising that Dr Davies was highly regarded. He was a joy to have as a doctor and his home visits were oddly delightful, however ill you felt. I would hear him grunting a bit as he negotiated the stairs in our house; then slow footsteps crossed the landing room where I knew he would be looking at the paintings. At last he would appear, stooping a little in the doorway. He would then sit down heavily in the wooden armchair near the window, on my side of the bedroom. He would relish a moment or two of quiet, recovering his breath and trying hard not to look at the bedroom bookshelves for any new titles before asking how I was progressing. Of course, he probably knew the answer to that. He never wasted time and would have been observing and listening already.

One day he called in and I sat up shakily, leaning against my pillows, and he burst into laughter. I knew something was funny, whatever it was! I also knew he was not laughing in an unkind way, but I really wanted to share the joke. I sat there wheezing, prim in my white Victorian night-dress, the one which fastened on the wrong side. Perhaps they were not so fussy in those days. Maybe he was laughing at one of the catalogue of jokes he knew.

Having examined me and prescribed his own special medicine, which he called 'Industrial Boiler Mixture', and which really did clear wheezy chests, he looked across at the books again. 'Please,' I said, 'tell me, what is so funny today?' and he grinned and started talking about some author whose books we both enjoyed reading, so I didn't get a proper answer.

Months later, doing some research into Victorian clothes, including nightwear, underwear, etc., I discovered the cause of his merriment. The day he called I had been wearing a shroud! It was extremely comfortable and I continued to use it for years.

Another day he called again to check up on my wheezes. Once more I was wearing a Victorian nightdress, very frilly. This time he looked at me and said, 'Oh crumbs! If it isn't Red Riding Hood's Grandmother!' and then, 'Where's the wolf?'

The first time I met Dr Davies was during the long hot summer of 1976. At that time we were only occasional visitors to Knighton, staying in a rented cottage on the Stanage estate, which then boasted a beautifully manicured lawn and tennis court. Late one afternoon the family was surprised, to say the least, to see Dr Davies' car veer erratically off the drive and come speeding across the lawn to where they were playing tennis. He leaned out of the open window and called, 'Where does that tall girl live – the one who comes down from London?' That morning my wife had seen Dr Davies at his surgery – which then sported a sit-on model railway which shunted children around his garden. On opening the front door of our cottage she saw him for the second time that day.

'Have you taken those pills I gave you?' he demanded.

'No,' was the first thing she had any chance to say.

'Thank God,' he replied. 'I could have killed you. Gave you the wrong ones!'

He then came in and was delighted to discover the cottage full of children's books which he claimed – outside of medical tomes – were the only books worth reading.

Later, much later, just before he was forced to retire at the age of 70, I asked him if he was sad about it, to which he replied, 'What do you think, boy? I'm just beginning to get the hang of it!'

When I was writing a television series about a mid-Wales coroner he told me a story he swore was true, about a doctor – near here – who went on holiday leaving a locum in charge, giving him strict instructions about a particular hill farming family that had a son who consistently forgot to take his medication. Sure enough, and tragically, a couple of days later, the locum received a call to say the son was dead and could the locum go up to the farm. The son was indeed dead and laid out on the kitchen floor. The locum, of course, sympathised and signed the death certificate as being some kind of diabetic attack brought on by not taking medication.

A couple of days later the locum was in the surgery when the undertaker called him to ask if he was absolutely sure as to the cause of death. 'Yes, of course I am,' the locum replied somewhat dismissively 'You see, the boy consistently forgot or refused to take his medication.' There was a pause before the undertaker asked, 'So, you don't think the four inch shotgun wound in his back had anything to do with it?'

I once asked Dr Davies what had caused the biggest changes around here. He thought a bit, then said, 'The EU grants that enabled farmers to build roads up to the farmhouses – and television. It stopped everyone being so isolated.' He then explained to me that when he first came to Knighton, there might be 12 or 14 people employed on a farm but there would only ever be one kitchen range. So, when a man got a bit old or was stopped from working by something like arthritis, instead of taking up room in the kitchen and around the range, he would take to his bed – sometimes years and years before he actually died. He vividly recalled visiting several men like this and almost without exception, when he arrived they would be sitting up in bed in their pyjamas, wearing a bowler hat, so that they could raise it and say, 'Morning Doc.'

After he had retired he came to dinner one night with a number of others. At some point I realised two of them had gone missing. I eventually found them in the garden smoking cigarettes. Way back then, like everyone else, we had ashtrays and normally they had no problem at all smoking anywhere in the house. I asked them what they were doing in the garden. Both of them were well over fifty at the time and sheepishly replied, 'We can't smoke in front of the Doc.'

One joke that he knew he was making (and enjoyed), I pinched from him and used in the television series. It was what he would say when he was about to do something really painful to a patient, like putting a shoulder back into place, doing a bit of stitching (as he liked to put it) or giving a particularly horrid injection.

'I'll tell you something boy; this is going to hurt you a great deal more than it's going to hurt me!'

I am sure I can say without any fear of contradiction that Dr Brian Davies was one of the most respected and best loved GPs in the whole of Powys. Working with him for thirty years, as I did, was a pleasure. He was a great doctor and a great human being.

His patients received fantastic care, and his knowledge of their background and family history was extraordinary; he also knew where every elderly patient in Knighton kept their backdoor key! Be it under a flowerpot or doormat, he always knew and could gain access.

We (the hospital staff) were always so glad to see him and knew he could cope with any emergency, sometimes in an unorthodox way, but it always worked. His wicked sense of humour could always diffuse a tense situation. I remember one night that a nursing assistant and I were struggling to give a poor woman a sedative injection to prevent her fitting. She was a very large lady, extremely strong and, because of her condition, extremely militant. We were definitely getting the worst of it, minus caps and plus scratches, when Dr Davies appeared, and between us we managed to sedate the poor lady.

Not content with that, Dr Davies sat with her, quietly talking, until she fell asleep. 'You run along,' he told me. 'You have plenty to do. I'll sit here.' And she was not even his patient!

Next morning when washing this lady, we discovered the doctor's glasses, complete with case, at the bottom of the bed. I rang to tell him where they were and his reply was, 'Glad you found them, but for God's sake don't tell the missus where they were!'

He was a great man, doing a great job, and we were so fortunate to work with him and learn from him.

I was a District Nursing Sister and Midwife for the border villages from 1963 to 1997. When working the villages of Brampton Bryan, Leintwardine, Willey etc. my colleagues and I were always made so welcome. There was discretion on cross border visiting and meetings, at which I was always included.

Dr Davies may have been officially a General Practitioner, but above all, he was a family doctor – there is a difference.

Telephone conversation on the night of the finals of the Nurse of the Year:

'Hullo, Woozie, Dr Davies here.'

'Oh, hullo Doctor. Why aren't you watching the finals of Nurse of the Year?'

'No need to, Woozie, I married her years ago.'

On ringing Knighton Surgery one morning for some advice: 'Good morning, is that Dr Davies?'

'Well I was when I b-----well got up this morning.'

I cannot speak too highly of his help and support. Years ago, in the days of the hippie commune at Leintwardine and Adforton lay-by, I was the midwife responsible and Dr Davies and his Knighton midwives were my lifeline. Having problems with a young lady, in advanced labour, from the commune, I rang Dr Davies for help. 'Put her in your car, gal and bring her up. She can have the baby delivered, have a good bath, some food and then either stay the night or return to the commune.' The young mother in question, I found out later, was the only adopted daughter of a Harley Street Consultant.

At one time we had an outbreak of scabies at the local school. Two of our children succumbed and had to be painted with a lotion every night. I was getting a bit concerned for myself as we had a small baby. 'No problem,' said the Doc, 'you can borrow my whitewash brush.' Ask a silly question!

No going to A.& E. with minor lumps and bumps, or a bit of stitching. They were dealt with before you could blink. There was no waiting around anxiously for test results, as these were phoned through as soon as he himself knew.

I could tell endless stories of his kindness. We all got so used to his unique ways and took them all for granted; but we were so privileged to have received his kindness and care. There will never be another like him, and no doubt the angels are benefiting from his company and wit these days.

It's not very difficult to think of all the kindness that Dr Davies has bestowed upon me and mine; more difficult to remember are the outstanding occasions. I frequently call to mind arriving here one Friday evening from Birmingham, for a quiet weekend at Garbett, with a whitlow on my finger. The pain was intense and in desperation I timidly knocked on the kitchen door at the doctor's, explaining my tale of woe. I was instantly admitted and taken through to the surgery, where, with a very sharp pair of scissors, Dr Davies cut the offending throb away, remembering to tell me to turn my head away before he dived in. He slapped a clean dressing on the wound and walked out of the room, returning immediately with a jar of honey. He applied some (not the jar) on yet another clean dressing (hang the expense) and said, 'What's good enough for the Egyptians is good enough for me!'

The next occasion was again one weekend (always a good time to worry a doctor) when the family were staying with us, including our three year old grandson. At 10pm he woke up crying (a rare event for Jeffrey), with a raging temperature. We washed him down with warm water and then phoned the doctor for advice. Without hesitation he said, 'I'll be with you.' Now, to be 'with you' is not five minutes in a car, but not only did he arrive in five minutes, and no-one, just no-one, could do it any quicker than he, but he approached the little patient in a quiet manner and I remember him saying, 'Do you like 'Sam Pig', Jeffrey?' and on being given the affirmative nod, produced from behind his back the said book.

I ask you! Need I say more?

As a teenager, I remember having a cough and mum took me to see Dr Davies. He went into his kitchen, mixed pepper with honey and sent me home with a jar of it. There was so much pepper that the cough was too frightened to stay!

During the early 1970s, dad's disease had progressed and Dr Davies had to attend him during the night about twice a week. He would arrive in snow, rain, hail, frost, whatever, wearing his pyjamas tucked in his wellies and a coat on top. Never too much trouble. Dr Davies was a regular visitor to our house at this time, as dad was getting worse and he always gave us hope. He was so positive and made sure dad was comfortable.

As one of the First Aid Team at Walter's Trouser Factory, I often had to phone Doc Davies for several reasons; mostly needles in fingers. We could take the injured down to the surgery, or if there was anything more major he would pop up and sort it out, always with a smile, a joke and at any time of the day.

For the last few years I have not been working on a Friday. Every Friday morning I would go shopping and almost always bumped into Dr Davies, who lived close to my flat. He would always start the conversation with, 'Are you the one?' He was asking whether it was me or my sister, who looks like me. If it was not for him, I would not be alive today. I was delivered by Dr Davies; I had a very difficult birth and almost died, but through his expertise and knowledge, Dr Davies saved me.

When I was twelve years old, I was run over outside my house and suffered considerable injuries, including severe head injuries, leaving me unconscious for several weeks. Dr Davies came with me in the ambulance to Hereford Hospital. I was told that I almost died in the ambulance and Dr Davies had to do a lot to keep me alive. But he did, and I am here today, fully recovered, thanks to him.

A year after this accident, when I had returned home, my sister was taken ill and mum called Dr Davies in the evening. He turned up in his slippers and pyjamas, thinking I had had a relapse. He was quite relieved to know it was Sian, and not me!

I hope that Dr Davies is remembered for the kind, generous and friendly man he was – and he was my saviour.

Dr Brian Davies was not at Llanidloes for very long, but whilst he was with us, he gave of his best to his patients. He was very witty, a good imitator and very kind; everybody liked him and he was well praised as a doctor.

When a much-loved aunt was very ill and dying, I went to see her and she told me, with much pleasure, that Dr Davies had just been to see her and that he would come and see her at any time if things got too bad; even if it was in the middle of the night. She just had to telephone and he would come over. (She died two days later.)

When I asked someone in Bucknell how his old father was, he said, 'You can always tell when you walk in the door if Dr Davies has been. It cheers him up so much.'

Our children, aged about six and four years old, had chicken pox. They had made a camp with rugs and turned the sofa upside down etc and Dr Davies came to see them. I said, 'Come on out and see Dr Davies.' They said, 'No.' He said, 'I will come in and see you.' He crawled in under the table and made it such fun for them, and they were soon laughing.

To illustrate his understanding of children, one of our boys when aged about six, was having stitches in his face, after having fallen off his bike due to going too fast. I said to Dr Davies, 'Do tell Johnny not to ride his bike so fast.'

Dr Davies said to the pale child, 'If I tell you to ride your bike slower, will you?'

'No, I won't,' said Johnny, not in a rude way, just as a fact. Dr Davies knew it would make no difference.

Next day, despite cautions from me, he was riding it as fast as ever; in fact, as fast as he could make it go!

Dr Davies told me how once he resisted strong pressure from a family who wanted him to certify an old lady whose continued existence, had become an inconvenience to them.

My younger daughter had a lot of warts on her hands. A great friend of ours, who was an eminent dermatologist, had tried a number of treatments without success. On one of our regular visits to Skyborry, we happened to mention this to Dr Davies.

'She must see the wart charmer,' he said.

We all piled into his car and he drove us to the Chapel Lawn Smithy. He introduced us all to the old blacksmith, who was then retired. He looked gravely at Jennie's warts, and then, taking the stub of a pencil from the fold above the peak of his cap, he carefully marked each wart with the pencil.

'They will go away in six days, six weeks or six months,' he said.

As a doctor myself, I had my doubts, but six weeks later they were all gone! Thirty years on, Jennie herself is a GP. I wonder how she treats her warty patients?

There was an occasion when Doc Davies had been up country and brought back a dead body to Knighton Mortuary, strapped in the front seat of his Land Rover.

Our youngest daughter had dry skin under her feet which was splitting and painful. Doctor Davies' remedy was to go off to the vets to get cows' udder cream (really works a treat!!) On a similar line I went to see him with troublesome warts – his remedy was to recommend a wart charmer up the valley he knew.

He was always prepared to come out and visit whatever the time of day or night. In the latter case he was usually in his pyjamas with some clothes hastily pulled on over them. He never bothered with knocking on doors or ringing bells – he knew he could always walk straight in.

A couple of years after our daughter had a serious accident which left her in a coma, he met her in the bookshop in Knighton and they got to talking about the fact that she liked cats. A couple of days later, a book arrived in the post for her with a compliments slip from his surgery – T.S. Eliot's *Book of Practical Cats*.

I witnessed his skill and ability to stay calm in a crisis twice – once at the birth of our eldest daughter in Knighton, when we both survived due to his skill, and again when the same daughter was knocked down on the Ludlow Road. He was the one of the medical staff who responded. He managed to get a drip into her and came in the ambulance to the hospital with us. On the journey we thought she had died, but with his skill he kept her alive – while I was desperate, he kept so calm and it gave me hope that she would make it. He was in hospital visiting her a couple of weeks later when she managed her first words and he was delighted!! One day, I was out walking and holding a hazel stick. I started to fiddle with the top of it with my thumb and hardly surprisingly, a splinter went under my nail. I cleaned it when I got home, removed the offending bit of wood and wrapped it up.

Several days later, it was so painful that I had to go and see Doc Davies. 'Come in, young man' (with which he always greeted me, even in my not so young years). After I'd shown him my wound, he reached for a pair of what looked like sharp metal scissors and proceeded to make a diagonal cut into the middle of my nail and the infected skin. I felt a sharp pain, and then almost instant relief. He did the same again from the opposite angle to form a 'v' in my nail and all the pus came out. The

Doc did this so quickly that I didn't have time to worry about how much it might hurt. He cleaned it and then smothered it in honey before wrapping it up. I felt much more comfortable due to his expertise.

He was also the only medical practitioner I knew, who could administer an injection so quickly that it was over before you realised what was happening.

My first recollection of Dr Davies was on Christmas Day 1959 when my Mum said, ' I think you had better get the Doctor because I think he is quite poorly.' We were talking about my son, Stephen, who was just ten months old. I was concerned because of the date. It was lunchtime and there was quite a heavy snow. The nearest phone was at our neighbours', Mr and Mrs Williams, Lloyney. However, I phoned up apologizing for the time and the date to be very quickly told 'I'll get the Land Rover out and will be with you very soon.' Within ten minutes Dr Davies arrived. He took one look at the baby and said 'It's a good job you phoned up because Stephen has pneumonia.' With that he pulled some penicillin out of his black bag, gave me the instructions about the dose and told me not to worry as Stephen would be as right as rain in a day or two; and then off he went in his wellingtons and Land Rover with several of feet of snow to plough through. I immediately thought, 'I like our new doctor. He is so down to earth.' We remained good friends for all the years he lived in Knighton. His kindness and humour was second to none.

Many years ago Dr Davies said to my Dad, 'Charlie, I think we'd better take that cyst off your head. I've got a locum here for a couple of weeks. Get Maggie to bring you down on Saturday at about 7 o'clock; surgery should be finished by then.' Duly I took Dad down, saying 'You're going to bang your head in one of the cow sheds and that won't be good.' (Dad was 6'3' tall!) While the operation was taking place Alison insisted I had a cup of tea with her in her lovely warm kitchen with some nice classical music playing in the background. When the 'job' was over, in came Dr Davies and said, 'Get Charlie a big glass of whisky because it's been a rough hour for him.' He looked at me and could obviously see I was worried and he said, 'and a tot for Maggie as well'.

No breath tests in those days or much traffic so at about 8.30pm Dad and I returned home in our little Ford van.

One day when Doc Davies called on Bernard, my brother, who was ill, he saw a full packet of Woodbines on his bedside table. He promptly picked them up and told Bernard he was taking them downstairs to put them on the Rayburn. 'And I don't want to see you smoking again.' He then turned to me and said, 'Are you still smoking?' I said, 'Just a few,' which was not true because, as I was a civilian working for the Army in Shrewsbury, I got them for half the price that you paid in the shops – no excuse, I know. However, my full packet of Senior Service went on the Rayburn too and he looked at me and said, 'And no more smoking for you either.'

From that day to this I have never smoked and I'd almost been a chain smoker until then. That was Dr Davies laying down the law! Only a few years ago, I reminded him of this incident, and he said, 'Did I do that?' but I was really grateful to him for his actions and told him so. Stephen (my son) and his friend David Maughfling had a serious sidecar accident in Leicester. Both ended up in the intensive care at the hospital, but eventually they came home a few days later. Steve felt not too well a couple of days after and went down to see Dr Davies who said, 'You've got a punctured lung; no wonder you can't breathe very well, boy. I'll finish surgery and then I'll take you up to Llandrindod Wells where I'll keep an eye on you.'

Steve said, 'Do you mind if I tell Mum where I'm going,' (I was working at the Walters Trouser Factory) 'because I know she's going to London?' With that here comes Dr Davies to explain what was happening and that I was to go to London and have a good time. He would look after Stephen and there was no need for me to worry. What a character and friend.

Upon returning home about 6.30pm from delivering meat on a Saturday night, the phone rang and it was Mum, asking me to pop up to see her to get a bit of wood out of her eye that had got lodged there when she was chopping morning wood. I immediately went up to see what the problem was, to find her holding a very bloody hankie over her eye. She could not open it, so I said that we must phone Dr Davies up, but she was concerned that it was late and Saturday; but as we all know, none of those things ever bothered him. He just said, 'Bring her down and I'll see to it.' He told me later that evening that the piece of wood had just missed the cornea but he was going to dissolve the offending piece of wood – which he did. You rarely had to go to A & E when the Boss was on the case!

Much later that night when he had the eye problem under control he picked up off his desk a very pretty paperweight and said, 'That's for you, Mollie.' I still have that very special gift on our mantelpiece today.

I could write about so many acts of kindness that they would fill a book. His thoughtfulness, especially his humour; skill as a doctor and the hair raising lifts when he was in a hurry; his fight together with others to save the Knighton Hospital; the loans of some of his funniest books, especially the 'Loo' book and how rich you were if you had more than a one 'holer' (loo). The list is endless. I can image him up there saying to Alison, 'What on earth is that silly old bugger writing all that stuff for?'

I arrived in Knighton in March 1987 and when I went to the surgery they let me know that my tetanus and polio vaccinations were out of date. I was ushered into the Doc's room and he vaccinated me and then put the drops directly on my tongue for polio. I pulled a face, as I had always had it on a sugar cube. He rolled his eyes, but in humour, and took out a large chocolate tin which was filled with dolly mixtures. This was my kinda doctor, and a small gesture like that endeared him to me straightaway.

Dr Davies was a wonderful man and our family will never forget him. He was such a character but more importantly a remarkable caring man. My son had whooping cough when he was a year old and was very ill. Dr Davies would be at our house within minutes of a phone call, usually in the middle of the night. I remember him arriving with an overcoat over his striped pyjamas and slippers still on his feet! That's how important his patients were to him. On leaving he would always say, 'Don't worry gal, just call me if he worsens.'

My father had a serious heart attack at home in Ffrydd Terrace. Dr Davies brought equipment from Knighton Hospital to the house and saved his life. He knew if he moved dad it would have killed him. What a man; we loved him.

Dr Davies was a very caring man who loved his job. He went out of his way to help people, and I would like to tell of his exceptional care as a very well respected doctor. My partner suffered horrendously for over ten years with cancer, but still went to work every day. He ran his own heavy plant removal business. He would call in for radiation treatment at Cheltenham – park the lorry and goods, have his treatment, then go on to work. Dr Davies always admired his courage and determination, and helped him so much to keep going, but back in late 1983 things got far worse. He was admitted to Cheltenham, and I went with him and stayed at the hospital. After a month they told me there was nothing more that could be done, so we decided to come home, although anything could happen at any time; our good friends came for us. As soon as we arrived home, Dr Davies rang. He had been contacted by Cheltenham. He said, 'We are here for you both with whatever support you need.'

He was as good as his word, coming out every day to see us, twice on Christmas Day. I didn't ask, you never needed to. He came, he knew what we were going through, medication on board, and if there was anything specific needed, back to Knighton he would go to fetch it. Later when I had lost my partner, I was sitting having tea with two friends, when quite suddenly the door opened. In ran Dr Davies with a box. He put it on the table and said, 'This is for you.' I was speechless but did get a thank you out before the door closed, and off he went up the valley on call. On opening the box, inside I found two baskets, one marked December with Christmas roses, the other February with daffodils, all in bone china, and I had lost my partner in January. I will never forget his wonderful work.

When Alan's Dad was really poorly with cancer, he had to go to hospital every week to have fluid drained from his stomach. If it hadn't been for the Doc, he would have had to travel to Hereford Hospital every week, but the Doc organised it with Hereford that I could take him up to Knighton Hospital for the day and Doc would drain it for him there. I firmly believe that it gave father-in-law a little extra time with us, because the travelling to Hereford really knocked him about for days afterwards, let alone the treatment. What wonderful memories we all have of the Doc, some happy, some sad.

When I was returning home to Brampton Bryan from work on my motorbike, a drunk driver ran me down at Walford near Leintwardine. I awoke in the middle of the road, with Dr Davies looking down on me, dressed in a dinner jacket and black tie. 'How many fingers, boy?' he asked. After the reply, which I cannot repeat, because I was all smashed up, he turned to my father, who also had turned up at the scene of the accident, and gave the thumbs up. ' He'll be OK,' he shouted. He then went on to my parents' house, to let mum know. The Doc was at a dinner party some twenty miles away when he heard on the grapevine that of one of his patients was down.

The Doc very often visited his patients even when they were off in hospital if he had occasion to be in the area. After that bike accident, he was visiting the Hereford General (that was). He popped to the Harriet Davis Casualty ward, to see me trussed up like a ?? and to advise me how to behave in hospital as a young man (you can guess the stories that he was telling me)!!! Also, how to get better.

After the Doc retired he still kept a great interest in his friends' and patients' healthcare. He was mostly known by his colleagues as the 'Boss'. On one occasion he visited my dad at Knighton Hospital, in his later years, with some red wine to help him get better. My father, Richard Whittington, who had also been a soldier, was told by the Doc that when he was born, his father held him up to the stars, a custom from the East.

The Doc always had time and encouragement for his patients. Debbie, being from the United States, one Christmas was feeling down and homesick. The Doc told her, 'The best medicine is a hug from the Doc.' He always had little remedies to help, especially with the little ones, like honey on a plaster to draw a boil, or egg white and cooled boiled water to stop the sh**s when teething. We have been very lucky to have known him.

4 Having babies

In 1978 I gave birth to my first daughter, delivered by the midwife, who said that it was good to be delivering a baby rather than lambs, as she had been doing all week. After she had taken my daughter off to be cleaned up, Dr Davies appeared in wellingtons and a green apron ready to stitch me up. Once he had gone, I asked the midwife why he wore wellingtons.

'Oh, he doesn't like to get blood on his shoes!' she replied.

A few hours later (these were the days when you could stay in hospital for a few days and enjoy the rest), I was allowed to have a bath. As I stood up to dry myself, I spied something hanging from my nether regions, and in a panic I called the midwife.

'What's this?' I cried.

'Dr Davies always likes to leave a long end of thread. Don't worry I'll cut it off,' she laughed.

In 1980 I gave birth to my second daughter and Dr Davies arrived, minus wellingtons, just in time for him to cut the umbilical cord. It was so engorged with blood that as he snipped it, the blood spurted out and hit the ceiling and ... his shoes. The midwife told me later that he was none too pleased, but he forgave me!

One evening in the spring of 1961 I was standing on Harris' corner with no other purpose than awaiting my evening meal at my digs in Ffrydd Road. Suddenly, the quiet evening silence in Wylcwm Place was disturbed by the screeching of brakes and tyres as Dr Brian Davies, in his little blue Ford Anglia 105E, came hurtling to a stop alongside me.

Knowing that I was one of Brisbane's part-time ambulance rota drivers, he instructed me to get in the car with him and he would explain. On our way to the Ambulance Garage at the Quarry, he quickly briefed me on the fact that we would have to attend to the business of transporting a lady to Copthorne Hospital in Shrewsbury, as she would shortly be giving birth.

Our next stop was up the Cwm, to the home of Roy and Sheila Powell (ex Bradleys), whereupon, we were greeted by the nurse and expectant father, who both thought that things would not be very long. After quickly loading Sheila into the ambulance I was instructed by Dr Davies to proceed to Shrewsbury with much caution, but at the same time with great haste. With the nurse in the back of the ambulance he assured me there was nothing to worry about and to quote his own words, which I have never forgotten to this day, 'If she calves on the way boy, don't panic, I'm right behind you.'

After stopping in Clungunford, Craven Arms and Church Stretton, we arrived fifty minutes later (the longest of my life) at the Copthorne Hospital. Within a very short space of time Sheila and Roy were the proud parents of a bouncing baby girl. After being thanked by Dr Davies for my service at such short notice, I proceeded back to Knighton in the BMC Ambulance and with an explanation for Mrs Smith, my landlady, as to why I was late for supper.

48 years on, I often think of Sheila and the little girl I helped bring into the world. The authority, knowledge and control of any situation like the one on that evening has always been the hallmark of Dr Davies' career, for which all of us in Knighton and District will eternally be grateful. We have indeed been honoured with the presence and devotion to duty of such a wonderful man.

One of Dr Davies' babies was my daughter Sarah.

A few years ago when Sarah was recovering from a fused disc operation on her back in The Whittington Hospital in London a voice suddenly said, 'What are you doing here?' and Dr Davies promptly gave her a bunch of flowers and wished her well.

We don't know how he knew about Sarah, but he was in London to give a lecture about medicine.

Our daughter was born in Knighton Hospital on the hottest day of the year in 1973. We hadn't a phone at the time so I was collected at about 2.30am, as the arrival was imminent. The baby did not arrive until midday, by which time I was completely exhausted with the heat and worry. The delivery was assisted by the Doc and Cheryl Cox, the midwife.

When it came to dealing with nappy rash we were recommended to use 'Sister Hamar's Granny's Bum Cream.' Very effective.

I was in labour up at Knighton hospital with my second child, Tracey, in January 1985, when things started to go wrong. I had a concealed haemorrhage and when my 'waters' broke it was nothing but blood. Luckily for us, Dr Davies was doing his rounds up at the Hospital and was having a cup of tea and cake when all this was going on. He came down and took over the situation, organising an ambulance and preparing me to go Shrewsbury hospital. He also came in the ambulance with us to Shrewsbury. All through the journey I wanted to 'push'; blood was gushing out, and every time I wanted to push we had to stop the ambulance.

My poor husband was following behind in the car, and with all this stopping and starting, he wondered whatever was happening. Anyway, as we reversed up to the doors of the maternity unit, I had lost so much blood that my body rejected the baby. I still maintain that Dr Davies caught her, because I had rejected her so quickly that she literally shot out. 14 doctors and nurses were then all around the ambulance, but Doctor Davies had wrapped her up and was fighting his way out of the ambulance holding the baby up in the air to get past, and that is what my husband saw as he was arriving at the unit.

They took her to special care and Dr Davies stayed with her until she was all wired up and settled. He also came in to see me to make sure I was all right, before going back home with the ambulance. Fortunately our daughter Tracey survived and we have great pride in the fact that this wonderful man, who was not our doctor, literally saved our daughter's life and became Tracey's godfather. We are so very proud to tell our story of this lovely, lovely man. He was also an absolute brilliant godfather.

Dr Davies insisted on being present at all the births of our five children, and became a well-loved, almost 'member' of our family. His speedy exploits had me ferried to Clun Hospital, almost flying in his truck, taking short cuts through 'Treverward', to arrive at the doorstep with matron wagging her finger in a state of alarm. Dr Davies just laughed. It was a good lark, a fun experience, but he was very caring and concerned.

At one time he even got a message to my husband on the fields of the army manoeuvres in Germany to let him know of the birth of his daughter.

My husband was by occupation an A.I. man (artificial insemination) for the then 'Milk Marketing Board'. Dr Davies always joked on the birth card written for each of the children – 'By A.I.'.

Whilst I was attending one of the ante-natal appointments before the birth of my first daughter, Dr Davies and I got talking about his keen interest in obstetrics. Taking the mickey out of my Midlands accent, he told me that he had recently had ongoing training at Dudley Road Hospital near Birmingham and could understand every word I said! 'I hated it,' he disclosed. 'The women were treated like goods on a conveyor belt, and moved on as quickly as possible. There seemed very little compassion.'

I know that as a new mum-to-be, I had been very nervous about giving birth in a small cottage hospital as opposed to a large city one, but the care and attention I received at Knighton Hospital for both of my confinements could not have been bettered, and it was all due to Dr Davies and his merry band of midwives.

When my daughter was one year old, she had a febrile convulsion and was admitted to Hereford Hospital. Dr Davies arrived soon afterwards to check if he could do anything.

When my son was born, Dr Davies arrived just after the birth, looked at him and said, 'Well gal, if anyone says his balls haven't dropped, they are wrong!'

Dr Davies delivered my first child in July 1979 (Friday 13th!), by what Pat Mercer, the midwife, described as the cleverest forceps delivery she had ever seen. 'If it hadn't been for Dr Davies,' she said, 'you'd have had the stress of being rushed to Hereford by ambulance with the siren wailing and the light flashing.'

His visits to his patients in the cottage hospital in Knighton were frequent – even on a Sunday he would come in from gardening, wearing checked shirt, dungarees and big boots!

Indeed there was no limit to the care he would extend to any of his patients in genuine need. One Sunday, when I had had my baby home for only a couple of days, noticing the little chap did not seem quite himself, I phoned Dr Davies just for some advice.

The next thing I knew, there was the doctor knocking at the door, coming to examine my baby, who, sure enough had a temperature. The distance from the surgery to our cottage was eight miles!

A friend of mine, while in the throes of labour, at her home in Presteigne, expressed a wish for a can of lager and lime, which were currently being given away with purchases of petrol at Brisbane's in Knighton. Dr Davies, ever eager to alleviate the suffering of his patient, drove all the way back to Knighton, and returned with the craved beverage. During her next labour, she tells me that Dr Davies attended ready supplied with lager and lime!

Dr Davies delivered me into the world, and my two brothers and two sisters. We were all born within six years of one another. Years later, he delivered my son Aled. Just as Aled was born, Dr Davies looked at me with the proudest expression and said, 'It's like playing with Russian dolls.'

Years later, Aled got a place in Mansfield College, Oxford, and Dr Davies sent him a £90 book token and a beautiful note of support. He also lent Aled books on history and a lovely wooden folding yard stick with all the major historic dates carved along the sides. When my daughter Rhian was little, he gave her a toy rabbit, which she still has.

We have great memories of Dr Davies, and although he was frighteningly honest, we felt safe in his hands, and enjoyed his wit.

When I was about eight years old, I had to give a urine sample, which was in a jam jar. Somehow, probably due to his erratic driving, the lid came off and it spilled in his car. For the next few years he always greeted me with, 'Ah, here's the little girl who peed in my car,' and would leave me to do the explaining!

Dr Davies pierced my two sisters' ears and mine. I'm amazed he had time for this extra free service.

When I went in to ask to go on the contraceptive pill, he telephoned through to Mrs Irving and said, 'Another one for a ticket to Paradise as she goes past, please, Doris.'

Always witty, always kind; I loved Dr Davies.

I visited Dr Davies in December 1975 thinking that I might be pregnant for the first time. In those days a sample was sent off to check, so the results were not immediate. On Christmas Eve, the phone rang and I answered it to hear a male voice saying only two words, 'You are,' after which he put the phone down!!

There will only be one Doc Davies. I first met him when I was a teenager seeking family planning advice, sometime in 1971, and he remained my doctor until he eventually retired. The most memorable event was when after waiting eight years to start a family, I went to him for a pregnancy test. Days later he strolled into the staff area of where I worked at Browns Bakery, and said, 'Congratulations girl, it's positive.' This was in 1979.

The next part of the story was when he arrived, dressed in his pyjamas and wellies, to help deliver our daughter. I had heard that this happened occasionally, but thought it was just another tale. Despite being fully occupied giving birth, I did glance down to see the pyjamas for myself.

He was the only qualified doctor in the area able to perform a forceps delivery. If it hadn't been for him, we would have faced a long journey to Hereford Hospital or suffered worse consequences. When I was about to be discharged from the hospital he said, 'Good luck girl, now don't go jumping any five bar gates yet.'

I was a patient of Dr Davies in the late 50s and early 60s. In 1964 I became pregnant!!! Eventually I had to accept the fact and go to the doctor's.

'I wondered when you were coming to see me. What are you going to do about this baby?'

'I'm going to have it adopted.'

'Best thing girl, leave it to me,' and leave it to him I did.

Any regrets? No, none at all. Thank you Dr Davies.

In 1977 I was a young wife of two years and I hadn't really had any dealings with Dr Davies, so I didn't know his ways. I went to see him for pregnancy test results. He didn't look up from his desk but said very matter of factly, 'Tell Sharpy he's scored a bullseye!' I could feel myself going pink. I'd never come across a doctor like this before.

Even though I had my first son in Hereford, before being transferred to Knighton Hospital, and my second son in Knighton Hospital while Dr Davies was on holiday, he still came to see us every day, at least once; they were still his babies. Over the years my children and I came to know Dr Davies very well. The children (31 and 29 respectively) still fondly remember the tin of dolly mixtures on the shelf for good boys and girls – not very PC these days!

I was in Knighton Hospital on the official opening day waiting for the birth of my second child. The Doc had been in to check on my progress on several occasions. At 7pm I was still waiting and the Doc arrived to tell me he was going to a dinner in Ludlow, but promised faithfully to be back in time to deliver the baby. He kept his word and arrived back at 11pm and Mark was born at 11.45pm, just making the official opening day.

Doc went home to put the house to bed and returned at 12.15am with tea and biscuits, sat on the bed, and proceeded to tell me about his younger days and how he and his rugby mates travelling back from a match lifted the hatch in the floor of the bus and took it in turns to relieve themselves onto a spinning cog below, to see who could spray the farthest.

A couple in town were desperate to have a baby, and after trying for such a long time the wife went in to Dr Davies for the pregnancy test results.

'Well,' said the good doctor, 'you can go home now and tell him he can take his L plates off.'

A lady with a lot of children went in for a pregnancy test, looked at Dr Davies and said, ' I am going to keep my fingers crossed for this one.'

He replied with a chuckle, ' Never mind the fingers – it's the legs you want to worry about.'

When it was time for our youngest son Paul to be born, Doc D. was there. He came into the labour ward at Knighton Hospital in a green apron and white wellingtons and said to Alan and myself that if he needed to go to the toilet he wouldn't have to leave me. He would just let it trickle down the inside of his apron into his wellingtons, so there was no need to worry. Things were progressing, so he lifted my legs up into the stirrups ready for the delivery, pulled the angle light down to be able to keep an eye on all that was going on and said, 'Ah well girl, we're on Nationwide tomorrow night'. Doc Davies' way of taking your mind off things.

The Boss delivered, with the midwife, my son Jon Whittington at Knighton Hospital, making sure that I was involved at every stage of the event. Debbie, Jon's mum, was told, 'Just get on with it girl.'

Later, when mum and baby were settled in their room, the Doc returned with a present of a little glass cat, and told Debbie, 'This little Whittington needs a cat.'

5 Driving mad

I was walking past Dr Davies' house one day when he came driving down, turned into his yard, hit the wall and took the back bumper straight off. He got out, picked it up, looked at me and said, 'I didn't want the bloody thing anyway,' laughed and went into his house. It all happened in a minute.

Although I've lived in Knighton for over 30 years now, it is a well known fact that unless your great, great grandparents were born here, you are a foreigner. But it was Dr Brian Davies who showed me all the hidden delights around and about these wonderful hills, and who thus brought me the familiarity of feeling at one with the landscape and a true part of Knighton life.

We would set off for a jaunt in Spring, as soon as the sun shone. For the first few years he was the driver. Every time he passed a familiar face, both hands would come off the steering wheel and they would clasp together over his head, accompanying the shout of 'Hey boy!' I would shut my eyes tight, grit my teeth but somehow we'd stay on the road.

I expect his car, which survived more bashes and dents than many others, had a full set of gears but he mostly favoured second, occasionally third, and we'd judder and lurch over many a hill, pausing occasionally in the middle of the road, while his eyes sought out an interesting tree or a standing stone or a blackthorn bush perhaps. The first primroses would be the reason for the outing one day, or a visit to a crumbling Abbey on a faraway slope, another. I learned the names of flowers and rivers and lakes and mountains, all the while listening to tales of the Afghan wars or his early years with his beloved Alison. Often he wore his favourite shirt, a bright red plaid. 'My pulling shirt,' he told me, 'that's what the girls in Prince and Pugh call it.'

Eventually and inevitably in later years he had to stop driving and most of Knighton quietly sighed in relief

And then he would navigate and I was allowed to drive. We'd stop for lunch in a pub. He'd always order exactly the same as I did. Then we'd head off again over the hills and across the river until we got to Hay on Wye, his favourite destination. We'd go into the Cinema Bookshop there and young and glamorous assistants would rush to greet him with a hug and sit him down in splendour with a cup of tea and a biscuit. However often I drive around, with whichever friend, child or grandchild, however many primroses I see in however many days of sunshine, no journey here will ever be the same again. Like so many, many others, I miss him.

One of the kind deeds we never forgot: My late husband, Harry, was having to go to Llandrindod Wells Hospital for x-rays. The receptionist would ring up from the surgery and tell Harry to be ready at a certain time and Doctor would collect him, always on time. They would set off, first speeding through Home Farm Lane, sending the fowl flying in all directions out of the way. Then the Doctor would proceed to call on his country patients, again speeding round the lanes and by-ways, up rough farm tracks, just missing gateposts, with Harry holding onto his seat in case he hit the car roof. They would often come away with a box of eggs and a chicken.

By the time they reached Llandrindod, safe in one piece, Harry would say he needed a bed not an x-ray. The Doctor would then bring him back safe and sound and say, 'See you next week, Harry.'

I also remember him calling on us one Saturday afternoon when we were watching the Welsh Rugby match. He stayed quite a while to watch, getting excited when they scored.

The last time I saw Doctor was when he was coming away from Wylcwm Street Surgery and we had a little chat, and he came out with one of his witty remarks. He said, 'I have just been for my M.O.T.' How we laughed. That was typical Dr Davies. He was our rock.

Like every family who were patients of Doc Davies, we have many fond memories. He was not only our doctor, but our friend. Through thick and thin times, he was there with his humour and words of comfort. His kindness knew no bounds; he was one of us.

I used to travel with him to visit Alison and my aunt in hospital, a journey, which normally took an hour – but not so with the Doc. We went at ninety mph across country, up and down lanes and would arrive in thirty minutes flat. The windscreen would be splattered with dead insects. On a wet day, you could hardly tell the colour of the car!

On one occasion we collided with a lime spreader. The poor driver sat in his cab like a mesmerised rabbit, as he confronted this character (I could not repeat what was said). But I thought quietly to myself, 'It takes one to know one.'

On another occasion, I had a late night call to go to Shrewsbury Hospital; my mother was very ill. I phoned Dr Davies and asked him if he would go and ask my aunt, who lived close to the surgery, if she would come and stay with the children, and tell her that we would come and pick her up as soon as we could rustle up some petrol for the car.

Ten minutes later we saw some headlights rocketing up the lane. A vehicle screeched to a stop and out jumped Dr Davies in his pyjamas and wellies and my aunt in her nightie – plus a can of petrol; he even offered to drive to Shrewsbury. Thinking back, I don't think we ever paid him for the petrol.

I once sustained a riding injury to my shoulder for which I was having physiotherapy at Knighton Hospital. Dr Brian Davies, who happened to be in the department at the time, heard me groaning as I tried to do the exercises. He whisked back the curtains and asked whether I had had an x-ray. No, I hadn't.

'Right, come with me, I'll take you to Llandrindod Hospital for one.'

'What, now?' I asked amazed, knowing that the usual procedure is to be told to go to the surgery for the necessary form to take to hospital for an x-ray.

'Yes, now,' he said.

'But I've left my husband somewhere in Knighton. He won't know where I've gone to.'

'Oh, we'll soon find him in Knighton. Come on.'

I found myself seated beside the doctor in his car. As we drove up Broad Street I saw my husband John, about to enter the bookshop, and called out to him to accompany the doctor and me to Llandrindod Wells, some twenty miles away. With an air of bewilderment, he got into the back seat. In our innocence we knew nothing about Brian's reputation for death-defying driving. What a pity, I thought, as we hurtled around the many dangerous bends, with Dr Davies looking back at John in the back seat, chortling with laughter, as they swapped witty jokes together, whilst I grew quiet. We've only just retired and come to live in this beautiful area and now we are going to die, for sure!

By a miracle we arrived at Llandrindod Hospital in one piece, although the pain in my foot, which had been pressed to an imaginary brake on the floor of his car for the entire journey, by now outweighed the pain in my shoulder. Dr Davies set my x-ray in motion, and it showed that I had not sustained a fracture. Good news, but wait a minute, there was the journey back to be negotiated and my blood pressure rose! Of course, I've lived to tell the tale. Dr Davies was the last of the old school of doctors, the like of whom we shall never see again, and Knighton is poorer for that.

My family home, The Dimmey, was across two fields. Dr Davies was called out, and he came bouncing up the fields like a rally driver, did a big 'sweep round' in the soft earth and left the wheels tracks there for all to see for months!!

For a few years I was a member of the Teme Valley Motor Club in Knighton and we had an annual big Motor Cycle Scramble held at the Graig Farm by kind permission of Mr Fred Bevan. Over the years the event attracted many top Motorcross Champions, sidecar and solo machines.

My first job (or June Price's) was to pop in to see Dr Davies to see if he would be available on a Sunday, to be our First Aid Doctor. There never was any hesitation. The Boss just said, 'I'll be there.' And he was. His only request was, as the scramble was approximately two and a half miles from Knighton, if he could have a 'runner' who would pop down to Alison to check that there wasn't an emergency at the surgery. Dr Davies also came up early in his Land Rover and toured all around the course to make sure he could get anywhere. Of course he did in record time if there had been a pile up, as there often was, with fast machines and top competitors. Everyone knew him and most of the riders too. This wonderful service and the Knighton Red Cross, worked very well together and nothing was any trouble to him. In fact, I rather think he liked the thrill of the speed, mud and water jumps.

Dr Davies was the medical officer for a car rally on the Beacon Hill near Llangunllo. He must have thought he was part of the event, as his car ended up on its roof!!

I was working at Brisbane's Garage when this Land Rover pulled up. Dr Davies got out and asked me to show him the controls for four wheel drive and low gear, as he did not know how.

If Brian Davies had a new car I could be sure that in a few weeks he would come to school and ask me to come outside and see his new car. On going outside I would see the car, which would have a dent or scratches along the side. He would say, 'Do you like the car? I've just christened it.'

My husband was in bed with gout and I sent for the doctor. Doctor Davies arrived. He went up to see my husband, came down and wrote the prescription and said, 'How are you going to get it?'

'I'll walk down.'

I live in Norton and it meant going into Presteigne.

'Oh no you won't, I'll take you,' insisted Doctor Davies. I shouted goodbye upstairs to my husband. My husband then said, 'Mind what you're doing!' Doctor Davies shouted up to him, 'What don't you trust? My driving or my morals?'

Doc Davies came to Knighton when I was six years old and was our family GP for forty years.

My father had been under the Doc's care for many years. One evening his condition worsened and the Doc was asked to visit. Doc Davies never knocked, he walked straight in. When he arrived he looked a little concerned and said, 'I've had a bit of trouble with your gate.' When we went outside, the gate was on the ground in several pieces and the Doc's car was parked in the middle of the garden. After he had a cup of tea, we removed the remains of the gate and he reversed his battered car through the space in the hedge onto the road.

We first heard of Brian Davies in the snows of January 1982 when we were staying in Little House Farm beyond Felindre and were cut off by the snow. After a few days we heard that a Land Rover was going from Felindre into Knighton. We managed to hitch a ride, leaving the car behind for a month, and met the husband of a woman from Beguildy who had been about to give birth when the road was closed by snow beyond Lloyney. He told us of Dr Davies' great feat in driving through the fields to get to Beguildy and back, so that the very pregnant mother was able to give birth in Knighton Hospital.

After our arrival at Upper Goytre in 1984 Dr Davies came up several times with a student to show them what kind of outlandish places you had to get to as part of the work in a country practice in the Welsh Marches. He insisted on coming up from Lower Goytre at the bottom of the hill, when Marjorie and Brian Hewins lived there. There is no track all the way up and he got stuck halfway up on one occasion in the rain.

There's a lovely story one of the farmers told me about someone who'd died on a farm on the side of a hill. It was wet, and the death was not expected. They called Brian out, and he went with a policeman, because someone had died in a house on their own up there. He said, 'We can make it' and in a Ford Anglia they went up this bank to get to the house. The locals said, 'Oh, I shouldn't do that if I were you, doctor, I don't think that motorcar'll make it.' And sure enough, as they went up the bank, the Ford Anglia started to roll, with this big policeman and Brian in it, all the way down to where these people were standing. 'I told you, doctor, you weren't going to make it, you know.' There's Brian upside down!

At Stanage Doc Davies went through a hedge and ended up spanning a stream with two wheels of his Hillman Hunter on one side of the bank and two wheels on the other!

He had a brand new white Landrover in the morning and by early afternoon he said he was happy now. When I asked why, he pointed out the damage to the near side mirror and scratches down the side!

He had a brand new Avenger with less than 1000 miles on the clock. He collided with a lorry at Beguildy and wrote it off!

In preparation for winter he would put breeze blocks, shovels, ropes, torches etc into the back of the Landrover just in case anyone needed a tow or any other emergency he might encounter. Both Landrovers that he had were modified so that he could get a stretcher in the back with complete survival kit.

There was a permanent scrape mark on the wall of the Horse & Jockey. As the Doc took off at speed from his surgery in Wylcwm Street, it was always the first bend that would catch his car!

6 All kinds of kindness

During Dr Davies' funeral service the wife of one of the local vets told me that if her husband was seen by Dr Davies going into one of the farms during the dark evenings he would follow him and offer to shine the headlights of his car to be of assistance!

There was a family who lived in Bucknell, and suddenly the wife became ill with a nervous disability and ended up in hospital. Unfortunately her husband, who was in the merchant navy, was away in Venezuela. There were two children, Sally, who was eight years old, and Andrew, who was six. We decided to take them in.

Dr Davies found out and came to see us. He said, 'Here's some money for you to get what is needed for the children.' He frequently called in to see how the children were and told us that if we needed anything at all we should get in touch with him.

Later, their father came home and the mother's health improved so that she could go home and the children could return to their parents. What a wonderful doctor, carer, provider and professional man he was.

In the summer of 1959, when our hens were not laying, my mother sent me to Park Cottage Knucklas to buy eggs from Mrs Jones. As I passed by the well and climbed the steps to the garden path, I heard a ewe bleating and a lamb crying. Kneeling by the woodpile by the back door was a man comforting the lamb as he applied a wooden splint to its broken leg. He returned the casualty to its mother on the other side of the garden gate. Rubbing the dust from his trousers, he came into the kitchen and washed his hands with carbolic soap. As I left with the eggs, I heard him say, 'Now I'd better go up and see the two-legged one.' On my way home I wondered whether it was one of Mrs Jones' hens or ducks which needed his attention next, and told my mother we had a new vet.

A short time later, in August, a group of us villagers were blackberry picking on 'The Scrubs', a steep rough piece of land near Heyope. Mrs

Nicholas, a rather fragile lady of advancing years, eager to reach the finest fruit, leaned over too far, stumbled into a rabbit hole and broke her leg. Someone volunteered to run down to the telephone kiosk in Knucklas, promising to hurry back to tell us when the doctor was coming. As we tried to make Mrs Nicholas as comfortable as possible, and long before the messenger had returned, we could see clouds of dust and hear the roar of a Land Rover. It bounced towards us and screeched to a halt. The door flew open and the driver ran towards us. He gently lifted Mrs Nicholas in his arms and carried her to the vehicle. As he rushed her to hospital, disappearing again in a cloud of dust, I realised that he was the same man who had been tending to Mrs Jones' lamb. He was not a vet but our new doctor.

Little did I know then that I would become the third of four generations of my family fortunate to be in the care of such a dedicated, caring, compassionate and generous man, whose wicked sense of humour was an extra bonus.

While playing with her sister, our small daughter fell awkwardly and dislocated her elbow. She was in great pain and very frightened. We rang Dr Davies' surgery. Mrs Davies told us that the Doctor was visiting a patient up in the hills but that she would contact him.

It was not long before Dr Davies arrived at the house. In no time the elbow had been corrected – accompanied by a sharp cry of pain! He told the girls that the best kind of treatment for this sort of problem was an ice-cream poultice applied internally. With that diagnosis, he disappeared to the village shop and was soon back with the 'prescription' in hand. Having helped himself to spoons from the kitchen, he sat down with all of us and shared the ice-cream.

The elbow was soon forgotten. Two much happier children. What a doctor! We shall never see his equal again.

Dr Davies often used to bring little treats when he called. One day he put his hand out to me and there were three sugar mice dangling from their string tails. I loved those, especially the pink ones.

I was teaching in those days and 'my' children were always glad to see what interesting or unusual items I had brought into school for making things. They turned bits and pieces into all kinds of things; junk treasures! There were the little cardboard rings at the centre of sticky-tape rolls, or some small clear plastic medical clips, which looked like miniature perspex tunnels. One day Dr Davies took about ten of these out of his pocket and spread them over the bedclothes. If you were very tiny you could have crawled through them. 'Here you are, gal,' he said. 'Some little glass cloches for you and the children to grow miniature lettuce.'

After his retirement we occasionally had lunch at the same table in one of the local tea-rooms and he always insisted on paying, which was so generous. These lunches were really rather quiet. Eating is a serious event, after all! Usually, just as we were leaving, someone would come up to him, or hail him from across the room.

'Hello, Doc! Remember my daughter, Lobelia? You know, you had a terrible time making sure she survived her delivery ...' and there would be grown-up Lobelia, looking bright, pink, plump and shiny, and as strong and tough as many a farmer's daughter has to be.

Then the Doctor would be reminded of the dreadful journey to arrive in time for the birth, or the fact that he had narrowly missed hitting the dog, cat or gatepost as he had arrived. Later on Lobelia would probably have shared sugar mice as well and would have great affection for Doc, as did her parents. As a child, Lobelia would probably have received a picture book, if she had been ill enough to have another visit from the doctor.

My children regarded Dr Davies as their great friend. When Sally was almost three years old, she went missing one wet and windy Sunday morning, along with her dolly's pushchair. We had the neighbours out searching. Panic was setting in on my part, thinking of all the terrible disasters that could befall her.

Eventually, she was seen in the company of Dr Davies walking towards home. Sally had such faith in him that she had wheeled dolly in the pushchair, down about eighteen steps, across Broad Street and around to the surgery to get Dr Davies to give her doll an injection, because only Dr Davies could make dolly better. The injection mark is still on the doll's arm!

When I had our next child, Dr Davies gave me an apple with the words 'An apple a day keeps the doctor away'!

Dr Davies was a wonderful person. When my son Geraint fell off his bike on the lane by Oakleigh in Whitton, Dr Davies put honey on his arm and said, 'It's the finest thing out.' I never heard any more about Geraint's arm.

When I had corns, he would get his knife and I'd say with horror, 'What are you doing with that?' He'd say, in his way, 'I'm going to cut your bloody toe off!'

Another day I was looking at his garden with him and I said, 'I like those lilies,' and he said, 'I'll keep you some.'

I never thought he would remember, but he did. One day I had a phone call, 'Are you going to be in, in the next half hour?' 'Yes,' I said excitedly, and he came around with lots of flowers, including those lilies that I liked so much.

On another occasion I saw him in the street and asked him if he liked blackberry and apple pies. 'Oh, yes. I love them,' he replied. So I made cakes and pies on a number of occasions and took some for him. He said that he used to love them. 'They were lovely!'

Dr Davies was a friend to everyone. He told us more than 25 years ago, that he knew where we lived; above the snowline. He was always willing to help, though he knew we were patients at a Herefordshire practice, having newly come to the Marches. Later on, he came up to visit us, bringing medical books he had bought for our son and daughter-in-law, who were volunteers abroad. He threw them on the table, covering it, and said, 'These are for the lad.' He quelled our grateful thanks with, 'It's nothing. I fall into bookshops the way a drunk falls into a pub.'

Going into Knighton was always spiced with the hope of meeting him. In answer to an enquiry after his health, he would say, 'Having a good time, though I shouldn't be,' or some other quip. He might be found in the bookshop or having morning coffee, or if at an evening event, doing the washing up and saying that we should be behaving well, as he was not; or walking up the hill, latterly with a stick, or crossing the road to get lunch. We learned to enquire at the Clock Tower Tea Shop if he had been in, because we felt we should leave the last Pavlova pudding for him, as it was his preferred sweet.

Tales abound about his visiting patients when needed, and not bothering about 'hours'; even driving them to the hospital in Hereford if there was no handy ambulance. And, of course, he was the main player in providing the maternity wing at Knighton Hospital. We all liked and honoured him greatly, and miss him in Knighton.

Over thirty years ago, I was living in one of the council houses in Llangunllo. I had reason to go to Dr Davies' surgery on a Saturday evening. As I was about to leave, he asked me how I was going to get back home. 'Oh, thumb a lift,' I said. With that he said, 'Go round to the house and ask Nancy (that was Nancy Felton) to make a cup of coffee and I'll run you home after surgery.' On the way home, he told me that he was cutting over the top to Lloyney, to break some news to a family there. I don't think many doctors would run you home after surgery!

Mrs Pugh, of The Bache in Norton, was unwell and Dr Davies dashed over from Knighton. Mrs Pugh had a hard life in those days, with a large family to support. Having attended to his patient, Dr Davies packed all the children into his car and drove them up to the village shop to buy sweets.

A doctor in a million, with many grateful thanks for his attention to my family over the years.

Whilst I was working in Broad Street on the launderette roof with Pat Pritchard, he suffered a heart attack. The Fire Brigade attended, but I felt a tap on my shoulder and Dr Davies said, 'How is he? Let's have a look at him and get him to hospital.' Nothing was ever too much trouble for Dr Davies.

During the 1960s, I lived in the country with my brothers, mum and dad, Milly and Tom Griffiths. My dad had Parkinson's Disease, was unable to work and so money was tight. At Christmas Dr Davies bought us a turkey, which meant we had a proper Christmas dinner.

We miss Doc coming in to see us, as he would call to visit us two or three times a day. Doc loved his Banoffi Pie.

Doc would leave his false teeth underneath his plate, and often forget them. Us girls used to chase after him, shouting, 'Doc, your teeth!' He used to turn round and laugh out loud.

Then there was the time that a little parcel was on the top of our cabinet. Everyone said that's for the Doc because we all thought it was sugar mice. We gave him the parcel, he opened it and guess what – no mice! Just his false teeth, which he had not missed!

Doc had his special place to sit in The Teashop and no-one would dare sit in his chair. All our customers knew which was one it was and it will always be known as 'Doc's seat'.

Then came the time Doc had live-in carers. He would walk up to The Teashop and we would ask where his carer was. He would reply, 'I have escaped,' and he would laugh, because they knew where he was and came in to sit with him. Us girls and customers miss Doc's laughter and humour. A void in our day.

I have a severe circulatory condition and used hand warmers which needed immersing in boiling water to activate them. When I visited on very cold days, Dr Davies asked for my hand warmers and placed them in the steriliser during my consultation. Then they were ready to use again when I left.

I expect other people have mentioned his special way of dealing with children needing vaccinations. He would come to the surgery door holding out his closed hand and beckoning to the child, saying, 'Come here, I have something for you.' While the child was investigating the sweets in his hand, the needle was in and out again so expertly that the child didn't notice until it was all over. Our children were fooled every time.

Dr Davies was a very generous and caring man who treated the whole body, not just the particular ailment. I was at risk of losing the use of my hands and every so often, a little gift would arrive which was some sort of craft item to keep my fingers moving. My fingers are damaged now but I still do a multitude of crafts and even run a craft group. All due to Dr Davies.

Our eldest daughter was experiencing problems about moving to secondary school and was very stressed. He quietly talked to her on her own and sorted everything out. During the talk he found that she collected owls. A few days later, a lovely macrame owl was left on our doorstep for her.

When I was young my father worked on the railway. One foggy night he was called out to work. On his way to Bucknell he was knocked off his bike at the Milebrook. Dr Davies was the doctor on call and he came out to attend to him. My father was not seriously hurt, but suffered broken ribs, cuts and bruises and was quite badly shaken up.

A few days later, although not our family doctor, Dr Davies called at our house to inquire about my father's condition, a gesture my family appreciated very much.

Many years ago a small group of ladies started a local group to fundraise for the Samaritans at Hereford. Alison, Dr Davies' wife, was one, and we often had our meetings at their home in Wylcwm Street. Dr Davies' job was to arrive at the right time to do all the washing up from these fundraising events. I well remember that he was most particular about having very hot water to rinse properly every item that had been used, and for this reason did not like germ-carrying tea cloths!

I have been told that if he was called to a patient early in the morning it was nothing for him to get the children who lived there their breakfast and get them off to school. He was a great friend to me and to the school and I could be sure that if a child had an accident in school he would be there in no time. I have known him come back from Llandrindod, take a child for an x-ray and take that child home afterwards. He wasn't just a doctor, he was a living saint.

When our house was flooded, Brian took us in at 3 o'clock in the morning, and by the time we got to him, the beds were warmed and the kettle was on. We stayed for several weeks, and for the nearly three months that we waited for the insurance company to replace our washing machine, Brian did our washing in his machine. If we didn't take any round, he would ring up to remind us – saying 'Dhobi-wallah here'. He couldn't resist saying that he could let it be known that he knew what colour Audrey's nighties were!

When Audrey's mother was taken to Hereford Hospital following a stroke, Audrey went in the ambulance with her, and was then stranded in Hereford as our car was being repaired. Brian lent Donald his car to come down to join her.

From time to time, he would enquire about the ages of our grand-children, and then produce presents of books suitable for their ages. A really kind and generous friend.

We met Dr Davies in Knighton. He was the other side of the street and he shouts over, 'Hey I was just going to write to you, see if you were still alive!' Talk about doctors today, he certainly would help anyone anywhere anytime.

I will never forget delivering meat for Al Marriott every Saturday and Tuesday to a Mr and Mrs Barnett in a little cottage in Felindre. The Barnetts had been rehoused during a slum clearance Government scheme and they were moved from Wolverhampton to Felindre. Sadly Mr Barnett died a few weeks before Christmas, and I never saw any relatives at their cottage when I called with a breast of lamb, which was the usual joint ordered. On that Christmas Eve delivery I saw on the table in the kitchen the most beautiful house plant I had ever seen and I said, in all innocence, 'Who's been spoiling you?' and she just broke down and cried for quite a long time before she could tell me that it was the Doctor, of course.

I also recall an elderly household in the Chapel Lawn area when three members of the family were quite ill, and who other than Doc Davies would visit with medicine and take their washing home with him and get it washed and ironed to be returned by the Doc when he did his round.

I clearly remember Dr Davies personally looking after Mr Jack Lock, a well-liked member of the Gypsy family, after he had been burnt badly in his caravan near Wigmore and he was brought to Knighton Hospital.

Many local people will remember the brothers Ray and Don Felton, who had their bakery in Church Street. Ray was very ill, too ill to get his wife a birthday present, as Doc Davies knew. We all know who turned up with a gift for Ray to give his wife.

7 Naughty!

From his boundless 'pharmacy' of personality, it wasn't a case of a spoonful of sugar to make the medicine go down, it was a spoonful of humour. Are we ever going to see his like again?

My husband and I were visiting our son and daughter-in-law in Knighton over Christmas. My husband had had an operation for colon cancer a couple of years before. However, he had not been feeling very well and he was in a lot of pain, so much so that the Doc was called on Boxing Day and he arrived and went upstairs to see the patient. The medical history was relayed and Dr Davies said, 'Let's look at your balls, then.' Despite the pain, it made my husband laugh, as he had never heard a doctor speak quite like that before.

A lady who was suffering from bronchitis and asthma sent for the good doctor. She was in bed with the pillow down in the bed and the covers over her head. He could just see the top of her hair. As Dr Davies walked around the room, he opened drawers and closed them. He then said, 'Come on then, where's the gin and meths?' At this remark she was quite cross and sat upright in bed. Dr Davies looked at her and said, 'That's better. At least I can see you now.' He was then able to sort out her problems and give her a prescription.

My funniest recollection (which you may not be able to print!) is when I gave birth to my son at Knighton Hospital in 1974. Dr Davies delivered him, lifted him up in front of me and said, ' He's OK gal, he's got two arms, two legs and two balls!! Ha Ha.'

Once I was constipated and suffering somewhat with piles, so I visited the surgery. 'What's the problem?', so I did my best to explain, without stressing that the piles were the result of being constipated.

He prescribed something for the piles and I duly got the ointment from Elwyn Roberts, but of course I was still constipated. Still in a lot of pain, I eventually plucked up courage and phoned the surgery, being far more specific about the root of the problem. 'If you can't shit, then just say so, ' was his blunt reply. 'Come down right now and I'll sort you out.'

On arrival he said he would soon put matters right with an enema, something totally new to me at the time. I asked him, 'How long will it take to work?' He replied, 'How long will it take you to drive up Presteigne Road?!'

I only just made it!!!

In 1966, when I was organising our wedding, I misdialled when phoning the vicar. The voice at the other end did not sound right and tentatively I asked, 'Is that Beguildy Vicarage?' A hushed voice replied, 'No madam, this is the Catholic Underworld.'

I was mortified when I recognised Doc's voice. To misdial is careless, but to disturb a busy doctor, unforgivable. I started to apologise but he interrupted, saying, 'Don't worry gal, you weren't far out. Try 252 for the parson.'

In the days when Peter Medlicott was Registrar of Births, Deaths and Marriages, his deputy was called upon to register a death. The usual medical certificate of cause of death was handed to the deputy registrar, who was unable to read it. The deputy had a problem. A bereaved informant was present. He had no choice but to telephone the doctor to ask what the certificate specified as cause of death.

He spoke to Dr Davies, who, in his usual impatient fashion, offered to come immediately to the Register Office. The Deputy Register presented

Dr D. with the illegible certificate. Contemptuously the doctor said, 'Any fool can see what that is – the trouble with you bloody lawyers is you can't read,' to which he received the reply, 'That's fine, but you bloody doctors can't write!' Brian Davies smiled and answered, 'Touché'.

My late wife and I were told this one shortly after we moved to Knighton. A respectable, elderly, chapel-going lady from up the valley went to consult the Doc.

'Go behind the screen and take your clothes off but leave your drawers on. Come out when you're ready.'

Some time later she emerges wearing a pair of bright red, knee-length flannel bloomers.

'Good God, girl, how long have you been playing for Liverpool?'

At the time we assumed that this was apocryphal but as we got to know him better we were not so sure.

At one time I had a cough and was told to go up to the Chemist and ask for some 'Little Black Buggers'. I overcame my embarrassment and asked. The description was good, as they were very small, very black and very effective!

Not long before he retired the Doc and I were talking, and he got onto some of his wartime reminiscences. He started to laugh and said that he was in a remote headquarters somewhere, when a crackly message came over the radio: 'Am bringing wounded English Officer down the river.' 'How do you know he is English Officer?' 'Easy. Every other word begins with 'f'!'

A gentleman who was suffering with long-term depression visited Dr Davies many times. On one occasion, the doctor gave him a piece of folded paper and told him to open this when he got outside. He went out, opened the note and inside it said, ' The best thing to do is go and find yourself a good woman'.

When one of my children was 3 years old he swallowed a ball bearing. I wasn't too concerned, but my sister was and insisted I phone the doctor, which I did, and explained what had happened. He thought for a moment and then in true Doc Davies style said, 'Don't worry gal, nature will take its course. Just don't point him at the window if he farts!'

One of the Doc's patients (a rather unrefined lady) visited him for an internal examination which he carried out, and in doing so caused her some pain. ' Oh **** me!' she exclaimed, to which he replied, 'Madam! I hope that's an exclamation and not an invitation'.

A rather well-to-do lady paid the Doc a visit, bringing her x-rays from Llandrindod Wells Hospital. The Doc studied them and explained to her the picture of her internal organs. She looked, and after a few moments she asked, 'And what are those black circles in my tummy, Doctor?' to which he replied, 'Those, madam, are your farts waiting to come out.' Exit one patient.

I met Dr Davies for the first time over nineteen years ago, shortly after moving to this area. He ushered me into his surgery and with that wicked chuckle of his said, 'Get up on the bed, girl,' and then added, 'The things us doctors can get away with!'

I last saw him two weeks before he died, sitting opposite me in the Clock Tower Café, eating his usual cake. I said, 'That will make you fat, Doc.' He stuck his tongue out at me and said, 'At my age, girl, who cares?' Such a wonderful man.

Dr Davies, when asked about his attitude towards alternative and complementary medicine, homeopathy and all that stuff, said, 'Well I'll tell you; there are some folk around here, if you told them to go up on the Beacon, at midnight, and dance naked in a circle, preferably on their heads, then most, if not all of them, would come back down totally cured!' Says it all really.

On one occasion, when I was a girl of fifteen or so, I was on my knees trying to light a fire in the living room. Dr Davies filled a syringe with cold water and squirted my back between my trousers and top. I was so shocked. He just laughed and said, 'I probably shouldn't have done that!'

The funniest story I heard about Dr Davies is that of the elderly country man who consulted him on an internal problem. 'Are you constipated?' asked Dr Davies. Then, faced with blank incomprehension on the part of the patient, he elucidated, 'Can you shit?'

I went to see Dr Davies about my constantly running nose, which was becoming embarrassing.

'Never mind gal,' he said, 'every healthy bitch has a wet, runny nose.'

My parents were patients of Dr Davies for many years. Dr Davies used to call Yoddy, my father, whose initials were D.I.G. James, 'DIG', and my mum, who was under five feet, 'TITCH'.

I worked as a Parish Priest in the Clun group of parishes, an area which included part of Dr Davies' patch. One day, I was visiting in one of the villages and was told that there was some concern about Mrs Jones (not her real name) because she was sleeping downstairs. Mrs Jones was a very 'proper' lady who was normally most particular. Bedrooms were upstairs and reception rooms were not for sleeping in. For her to have abandoned her rule, something must be badly wrong. However, the village knew that she would be furious if she discovered that her neighbours had asked the doctor to visit her, so they asked me to ask him. I did so and Dr Davies promised to include her amongst the elderly folk he called on as a matter of routine. The next time I was in the village, I heard the story which went something like this ...

The doctor found that Mrs Jones was sleeping downstairs because the soles of her feet were so painful that she could not climb the stairs. When he examined her feet, he found them to be badly swollen and infected. Having released the pus and bandaged her up, he asked what she had been doing. She produced a jar of ointment containing 10 times the amount of salicylic acid normally used in medicine. 'Where did you get this?' he asked.

'Oh Doctor,' replied Mrs Jones, 'I found it in the *Ludlow Advertiser*. It's a lovely paper, the *Ludlow Advertiser*. Do you read it, Doctor? You see, I wanted to buy some roses and I saw the advert for the ointment when I was looking.' Looking closely at the label, Dr Davies saw that the ointment was only to be applied for three days. When he asked her about this, she replied, 'Ah, but whoever heard of anything doing you good in three days?'

When the good doctor was about to leave, she asked him, 'Would you look at my roses, Doctor? You see I found them in the *Ludlow Advertiser* – it's a lovely paper is the *Ludlow Advertiser*, Doctor – and my nephew bought them for me. You see, I wanted roses that will grow up the wall. Do you think these will grow up the wall?'

At this, the Doctor exploded, 'Mrs Jones, if they are your roses, they will certainly grow up the wall! You are enough to make ANYTHING grow up the b- wall!'

I was informed that Mrs Jones had been told that the Vicar had sent for the doctor. Consequently, I knocked on her door with some trepidation – after all, the doctor had sworn at her! Fortunately, the relief that Dr Davies had brought to her feet outweighed all else and she simply thanked me for my kindness.

After my daughter was born, my mother came to stay to 'assist' and promptly went down with a dreadful stomach bug. Dr Davies was called, and quickly arrived. He had never met my mother before. She was a polite, well-mannered lady and was somewhat surprised as he approached her with a hypodermic needle and declared that 'The last time I used this was on an old cow'. She laughed about it for years afterwards.

On a visit to Dr Davies, regarding my development of prickly heat at the end of my holiday in Minorca, he told me he had suffered with that during the war. 'I used to cure it,' he said, 'by standing naked in the cool tropical rain. But I think you would prefer something more conventional.'

When I first came to Knighton, Dr Davies rang and my wife answered the phone. He said, 'Is your old man there?' and my wife, not knowing who was calling, said, 'Do you mean Mr Davies?' He answered, ' How many old men have you got there?'

I went to have my ears syringed at one time and as he was about to start, his partner, the late Danny Bevan, came into the room. He said to Danny, 'Don't stand there or you'll get wet, as the water will come straight through.'

Another time I went to have a 'flu' injection, and after giving me my injection he prepared another. I asked him what the second one was for and he said, 'You are going to give me mine.' I gave him the injection and when I pulled my shirtsleeve down there was a spot of blood on my shirt. So he went into the corridor and shouted to Danny Bevan, 'Come and let Dai give you your injection; he draws less blood than I do.'

I went to see him as I had pains in my neck and he asked me to lie face down on the bed. He leaned heavily on my neck and asked if that was any better. When I replied that it wasn't, he said, 'It can't be that, then.'

After hearing some of Brian's stories of doctoring 'up the valley' in the early days, I said 'Brian, you should put all this in a book.'

'Boy', Brian replied, 'if I did that I would have to leave Knighton.'

BCD and Mrs Burgoyne, NHS celebrations August 2008

8 Knowledge of many things

The Doc had universal interests and a oneness with the natural world. I have very precious memories of an afternoon spent with him when he was about to lose part of his lovely garden, which he enjoyed so much, so that the car park could be enlarged. I was just one of many invited to give his beloved plants a new home. As he dug them up for me to pack in a cardboard box which I has been instructed to bring, he explained which situation and soil they preferred. He stopped digging to point out a tiny firecrest which had perched on a bough. He was pleased to find ladybirds and careful not to cut worms in half. 'We'll wait for him to get out of the way,' he said. He delighted in telling how a visiting hedgehog he fed had put weight on after being so thin. He then went on to explain how his neighbour, Mrs Gill, told him that she too was also feeding a hedgehog and how pleased she was that it was gaining weight. Then one day he noticed 'his' hedgehog going through a hole in the wall to have a second feed on the other side!

Pausing and leaning on his spade, he noticed a faint moon in the blue sky. It reminded him of night visits to the upper reaches of Elan Valley, when practising in Llanidloes. Returning home on moonlit nights, he would stop to look at moon rainbows. These he explained are colourless and formed only when the moon is the only source of light.

We continued collecting plants: bearded irises, 'very posh', and mullein, 'they have babies all over the place, can't stop 'em'. As I write, Doc's irises are sending up new leaves and the first mulleins have appeared. 'In the summer, when they are standing tall and straight,' Doc explained, 'the mullein moth sends all her caterpillars up the stem. They are pale blue with black spots and yellow bands and taste so bad no bird will eat them. So you will have hundreds of the little B ... s, who will eat all the leaves in no time.' As usual, he was right.

He was known as an avid reader and his car must have known its way to the enticing bookshops at Hay-on-Wye and other places. Apart from his patients, books were his passion. We shared wonderful hours (when he was off-duty, later on) looking at his latest haul from the second-hand bookshops. He found the most amazing old medical books. The quality of the print and the detail of the drawings were fantastic. We wondered at their beauty and the skills of the illustrator and the quality of the paper. In this situation I was often the pupil and he the teacher. We spent ages discussing how some of the very early anatomical illustrations could have been made. Gruesome to think of dismembered corpses and the experiences those early ancient artists endured for the sake of spreading knowledge.

Another area we talked of and read about was the treatment of prisoners in days gone by. We had many discussions about social attitudes of earlier centuries. I was able to read, from the writings of people who lived then, about infamous prisons, and Bedlam where the mentally ill were detained, which was almost too horrible to think about, but is sadly part of our history. We were both disturbed to read that people, indeed whole families, went to visit such places just to watch the inmates. It was thought of as an afternoon outing. Thank goodness, we said, for Elizabeth Fry, and others after her, who tried to change things for the better.

It may seem odd but the good doctor was quite an expert about the history of nursery rhymes, of which there have been many, but now our folk memory and social attitudes have changed much of that. Nursery rhymes, if selected wisely, are a wonderful way of learning history, and not just that of the British Isles. They cover much of the world and give glimpses into a past we would otherwise forget. It may seem hard to believe, but the doctor and I happily shared books of nursery rhymes, which had weird and wonderful illustrations made when printing was done by hand. We would be deep into the mysteries of 'Ding-dong-bell' or who was Mary, who 'had a little lamb'? when the phone would ring. He would have to dash off immediately, so Alison and I would have a cup of tea together, and talk about the boys or the weather or how things were in the garden ... At least, that's how it was in the early days, until sadly Alison died.

After that life had to go on for him, and I fancy that the book-buying increased, discussions became more diverse, and the local cafe became even more important, perhaps even a kind of refuge for him, a place to see familiar faces and feel at home in a different way. He was always assured of a warm welcome from somebody and they kept his own special coffee mug at the ready. Did his own mug have a pig on it, as it does in my memory? Quite appropriate for one who must have known the rhyme, which mothers played with their babies' fingers and toes, about 'This little pig went to market'.

It seems to me that whenever I had a question he was always able to provide an answer and, frequently, would lead us up another mental pathway to reach an even more interesting interpretation of what we were exploring at the time. To work with someone of the doctor's intellectual calibre and experience was a privilege, even though I knew that if there was ever an argument, I would never have won! I have to say I treasure the hours I spent with him and his family, relations and friends. If he were here now I would say to him, 'Do you remember the Winnie the Pooh stories and all Rabbit's friends and relations?' Visiting the house was a bit like that at times, and there was always 'Owl' to turn to for advice.

One amazing winter's day I had just driven down the A49 from Shrewsbury and walked quickly to town, to see my husband at the antique shop near the centre of Knighton. There was a flurry at the door and in walked the doctor. 'Come on, gal' he said. 'You've just got to go where I have just been! You will never see anything like it again, you must come.'

I knew that the Land Rover should be safe on ice; so remembering its four-wheel drive, I went. We whizzed up to the hills above Llanfairwaterdine and Bucknell. It was true! I would never forget the exquisite, unexpected and curious visual magic of that freezing cold day. There were breathtaking vistas as the ice sculptures that were frozen crops stood with sun reflecting coloured light about them on the steep slopes. Jewel-like icicles hung from the bars of gates or the corners of barge-boards, changing the whole character of the landscape. All around was the mysterious, breathless quiet of the hills. It was the sort of day that was almost too beautiful to write about. Wales is like that.

In later years a friend and I would call in on Sunday mornings, on the way home from church. The doctor, long retired, would be sitting in his chair, snoozing or chatting with his carers. He was still buying books for schools, for children he knew, and for those who might need something useful for their academic researches. Many of these young people had been delivered to their exciting and challenging world by 'Himself', as some of us called him. He was always a great encourager and never, ever ceased giving in his unique and generous way.

He took pleasure in achievements, of whatever kind, and knew much about the struggles behind so many lives. He was always thoroughly professional, even when moved to tears about some incident or a memory which saddened him. Doctors always carry a lot of hidden sorrows and he was no exception.

Dr Brian Davies was a person difficult to forget. I will never be able to express adequately how grateful I am to him and his family for what they have shared with me over the years. We might acknowledge that our doctor could be obstinate and could be bluff, but get him talking about his life and books and medicine and he was vibrant, lively and happy as he used to be when fulfilling his onerous duties as our Chief Carer.

We have been so fortunate, and probably everyone will have gained from their encounters with him in some way. Old-fashioned values still count, and, as he knew, life must go on, and memories linger long.

We shared his passion for the Cadfael novels and we were delighted to find a complete set in the Bleddfa art gallery, all with Dr Davies' stamp inside. This led to a longstanding exchange of books with Brian. He introduced us to the African novels of McCall Smith and the nature books of 'B.B.' He also showed immense kindness to our disabled son, Thomas, supplying him with a variety of animal books, which Thomas loved.

He could not abide pretentiousness, and his manner could be brusque, but he was essentially motivated by true concern for his fellow human beings, which included a special respect for women, with the duties they traditionally bear. In spite of a love of literature, he could not forgive the poet Wordsworth for abandoning a woman who bore his illegitimate child in France.

It would be true to say that Dr Davies was my favourite customer. He has visited us regularly for as long as I can remember. We'd sit together, share a cuppa, and he'd often tell me a story, reminiscing about his time in the war, stories of his time in Knighton and Oxford, his family and friends. Interestingly, though, it was through his extensive book purchasing that we truly got to know about his family and some of his friends. His eldest grandson was doing a photography degree in Brighton; he got the Oxford Encyclopaedia of Photography. His daughter-in-law was studying Landscape Gardening; she was the lucky recipient of key works published by the Royal Horticultural Society and the like. His nephew's wife was, I believe, a keen worker of stained glass; again books were purchased depicting stunning examples of stained glass. I understand that Doris's husband used to work as a signalman. Dr Davies bought for him, amongst other titles, 'Our Home Railways'. The husband of his sister was I believe a potato inspector. He is in possession of some early interesting agricultural works. Dr Davies occasionally used to assist at the local school after his retirement. A full set of Thomas the Tank Engine, as well as many other children's books, were accessioned into the Knighton Primary School library, courtesy of Dr Davies.

What would Dr Davies' purchases for himself reveal? Well, he had enormously wide ranging interests, as one would expect from such a learned man. He purchased many books dealing with local history, folklore, military books relating to the Gurkhas and the North-West frontier in WWII. His medical library was extensive, and of course contained many important medical works relating to his key interest, midwifery.

However many books Dr Davies purchased, and as Mrs Davies would have testified they ran into thousands from us alone, it would only have been by sitting with him that one could have appreciated what a truly wonderful, kind and caring man he was. He is sorely missed.

I was visiting a friend, and Dr Davies was just leaving. We exchanged greetings and during the course of conversation I said I couldn't find many books about Knighton. A few days later a parcel arrived at my house with three Knighton books with a handwritten postcard which still acts as a bookmark. Thank you again, Dr Davies.

Last time I saw 'The Doc' was 16th December 2008, again visiting Knighton. He was going along by Boots. We caught him up around the corner, and said hello, and I reminded him about the books. He introduced us to his 'little sister' then said, 'Get out of the way or I'll fall down.'

That was the Doc, straight to the point; fond memories, indeed, of a lovely, lovely man.

I was completely stuck to know how to spell a certain word in an important letter. There was only one person to ring because my family were out and I could not find it in the dictionary!

Many years ago, Idris and I were going to walk to the source of the Severn and had been talking to Dr Davies about it. With that he promptly went into his home to loan us the Ordnance map for that area.

He was a real benefactor to Knighton Primary School and most of my early School Library was made up of books given by Dr Brian Davies.

When I was visiting the surgery one day, he showed me a set of very good history books he had bought. I was impressed with these and said that I intended ordering them. At teatime that evening we had a knock at the door. I opened the door and had a brown paper parcel thrust into my hands. It was Brian Davies and he said, 'I can't stop, I'm late for surgery.'

He had been out in the afternoon and bought the set of books for the School Library!

Brian was an active member of the History of Medicine Society of Wales and was always a delight to meet.

I have three vivid memories of Brian at Society meetings, always accompanied by his close friend Robert Irving. Their arrival at meetings together was a great joy to me. I first met him with Robert Irving at a meeting in Swansea Hospital over ten years ago. On arrival, they found that the meeting was being held on the first floor and there was no lift available. My heart sank at this difficulty but I did not have to worry as they gamely made their way upstairs, Robert with the help of his walking stick. They seemed undaunted, at the end of a successful enjoyable meeting, to face the long drive back home.

The second time was at a meeting in Llangollen in 2004 when my husband was President.

He had invited a colleague to tell the Society about her experience of working for 30 years in a mission hospital in India. The Professor told such a moving story that she brought tears to the eyes of hardened senior doctors but when she made a plea for donations to the mission it was Brian who quietly gave her the largest donation – £1,000. Later, the Professor went to her hotel room and when she realized how much he had given her she wept, knowing how many children would benefit from the money.

The third and last time I saw Brian was at a meeting in Narbeth in the autumn of 2007. It was an afternoon meeting, and Robert and Brian arrived just in time for lunch. I invited them to join us at our table and they were so happy to be there. They enjoyed the afternoon and set off for home at tea time.

A few days later I received a lovely bouquet of flowers from them as a 'thank you' for looking after them.

I did not know at the time that this was to be his last meeting. I have photographs of the lovable pair in Narbeth and of the flowers that I will always treasure in memory of Brian. He will be greatly missed by the History of Medicine Society.

I got to know Dr Davies in the last few years of his life. I was running a village bookshop in Herefordshire, and soon noticed that I had a particularly regular customer. He would buy armfuls of books on all kinds of subjects; loved books for children but was cheerfully rude about anything intellectual or philosophical. If asked how he was, he would say, 'Pig-ignorant but happy with it'. Before long, his visits included, in the winter, cup of teas, and in the summer, ice-creams which he'd buy from the shop next door. Sometimes he'd lure me away for a lunch-break soup at the cafe down the road, and sometimes, after hours, he took me driving ... I remember a trip into the hills above Hay to Llanthony Priory and a journey to the lovely chapel at Rhulen. He confided that he often used to stop there for a quiet moment on the way home from visiting his wife in hospital. As we left the chapel he stuffed banknotes into the collection box, and I imagined the churchwarden mystified by such generous donations. (I also remember our close encounters with the hedges on the way back.) He told me that when he was courting his wife he gave her a copy of *The Wind in the Willows* illustrated by Arthur Rackham, judging from her response to the gift that she was 'the right sort'.

He used to bring things – toys for my small nephews and some remarkable antiquarian books about Orkney when he discovered that my father was Orcadian. And of course I got to know the literary tastes of his friends and family; any passing hint from anyone about their interests would be another opportunity for him to express the generosity that was clearly second nature to him.

He often spoke with anger and frustration about the changes in the National Health Service which meant that doctors no longer attended their patients at all hours of day and night, as he had done. He was good-humoured, though, at the irritations and discomforts of increasing age, and relished reporting his various mishaps and near misses – the time when, for example, losing his way in the fog, he drove through a gateway and bounced through the fields until, luckily, he encountered a tractor whose driver helped him out of trouble.

During the years I knew him, his memory for the distant past became ever clearer. He loved reminiscing about doctoring in the wilds around Knighton, about how a pub landlord would round up regulars at the bar to stretcher a patient from some remote cottage without access by road. 'Is it a carry, doc?' the landlord would say. A very happy memory was of a time the doctor drove an ambulance all the way to Oxford, his only regret being that he couldn't work out how to set the siren or the blue lights going. Sometimes, remembering a medical story with a dreadful ending, he would cry; but more often, he would laugh and laugh, especially if the story had a naughty twist.

Going further back, he was full of memories of his times in the war – how much he'd learned as a very young and naive officer from the Welsh soldiers under his command, his disgust at observing how an American officer treated a black soldier on a railway station in India. Again, tears were never far away; he was especially distressed to remember events in Burma.

He often quoted snatches of poetry, and I enjoyed searching the shop's collection to help him remember them. He would quote Housman:

> Oh I have been to Ludlow Fair,
> And left my necktie God knows where.
> And carried half way home, or near,
> Pints and quarts of Ludlow beer.

But he loved Kipling above all, and one poem in particular seemed to mean a lot to him, though I never asked why, and now can only guess:

> I never sailed the Amazon and I never reached Brazil,
> But the Don and the Magdalena, they can go there when they
>   will,
> And weekly from Southampton great steamers white and gold,
> Go rolling down to Rio, roll down, roll down to Rio,
> And I'd like to roll to Rio someday before I'm old.
>
> I've never seen a jaguar nor yet an armadill-o,
> Dillo'ing in his armour, and I s'pose I never will,
> Unless I go to Rio, these wonders to behold,
> Go rolling down to Rio, roll really down to Rio,
> And I'd like to roll to Rio someday before I'm old.
> Yes I'd love to roll to Rio someday before I'm old.

My favourite memory of Dr Davies is of the time he agreed to open my art studio at Lloyney Mill and made the most marvellous speech. Here is what he said:

When Wendy asked me to open the exhibition of work done by herself and her collaborators, I didn't know much about what she was up to and decided to come and look. I was astounded and delighted with what I saw, work by amateurs of all ages and a host of different subjects and styles. The only common factor in all the exhibits was that they radiated enjoyment.

The Book of Proverbs Chapter 30 Verses 18-19 says: There be three things which are too wonderful for me, yea, four which I know not: The way of an eagle in the air; the way of a serpent upon a rock; the way of a ship in the midst of the sea; and the way of a man with a maid.

To these four we must now add a fifth: and the way of Wendy's people with a paintbrush! Quite apart from the actual pictures produced, this venture is, in my mind, immensely valuable in two big ways. Firstly, it gives people a chance to get away from routine bread and butter work

The Lloyney Mill launch

– vital though that is – and to create something of their own which bears the imprint of their own inimitable personality. We have all at some time or other paused at the end of a day's work and thought, 'Yes, that's all very well – it had to be done – but what have I personally achieved that couldn't have been done by anyone, or even a robot?' Wendy's venture offers an escape into a field of personal achievement, however small and inexpert, and that has a worth beyond price. Secondly, the venture encourages the development of vision, not just of seeing mechanically as in reading a car number plate at 25 yards but coming to understand how things in the world about us relate to each other and of their values. This seems to be more important still in children who are learning to live in our world and in society. A failure to develop this ability can be catastrophic. If 1 may revert to Proverbs Chapter 29, verse 18, it says: 'Where there is no vision, the people will perish'.

Last photo of Dr Davies, Christmas Day 2008

List of contributors

Anon

Baker, Roy
Barker, Peter
Basten, Richard and Gillian
Bebbington family
Boddy, Joyce
Bodenham, Janice
Branford, Christine
Brick, Jo
Brook, David
Bufton, Davina

Cinema Bookshop, Hay (Debbie)
Clayden, Paul
Cleland, Dr Philip
Creed, Anne

Davies, Dai
Davies, Sue
Davies, Sylvia
Davies, Wendy
Dowson, Alfred and Nina

Eaborn, Gladys
Evans, Dr Barry
Evans, Dr Trevor
Exworth-Dent, Fay

Fisher, David

George, Yvie
Green, Donald and Audrey

Harley, Susan
Hawkes, Clare
Hawkes, Linda
Hodnett, Janet

Irving, Doris

James, David
Jerman, Gwyneth
Johnson, Karen
Jones, Brian
Jones, Douglas
Jones, Dr Margaret
Jones, Sue

Kelcher, Edmund
Kitchen, Brian and Margaret

Lloyd, Idris and Margaret
Lockey, Mike

Matheson, Bill
Matthews, Doreen
Maughfling, Mary
Mee, Jocelyn
Minton, David

Neilson, Alison

Oliver, Rick and Carole

Price, Sheila

Reid, David and Brenda
Riordan, Christine
Roose-Evans, James
Rowlands, Christine

Sadler, Ron
Sharp, Sandra
Smith, Peter and Ann

Taylor, Kay and Elinor
Thomas, Jo
Tomlins, Geraldine
Townshend, Richard
Turner, Bernard

Vallance, Margaret

Whitefoot, Alan and Rose
Whittington, Debbie and James
Wilding, Mary
Williams, Beth
Williamson, Margaret
Wilson, Susan
Wozencraft, Anne